Going Home

Going Home

Donald S. Fortner

Go *publications*

Go Publications
Gibb Hill Farm, Ponsonby, Cumbria, CA20 1BX, ENGLAND

© Go Publications 2018

British Library Cataloguing in Publication Data available

ISBN 978-1-908475-11-4

Printed and bound in Great Britain
By Lightning Source UK Ltd.

This book is dedicated to:

Pastor H. Rondel Rumburg

A dear friend by whose example I learned from my youth the necessity of studious preparation for the pulpit.

Contents

Foreword

In sixty years of preaching and pastoring several churches, I have never been asked to write a foreword to a new book. Well, now that has changed. Yet, when Brother Don Fortner asked me to write the foreword for *Going Home*, I thought, "How ill-qualified I am to undertake this task!"

But what a delight it has been. These seventeen chapters are all about heaven and this is the best book I have ever read on the subject. As I read the fifth chapter, "Heaven: The Place of Satisfaction" my heart was blessed indeed.

Pastor Fortner does not tell us how easy it is for everyone to get to heaven. Many appear to think they can crawl through the eye of a needle! They imagine they will make it to the front row of heaven yet their lives give little encouragement to hope they know anything of the grace of God or the God of glory.

Instead, the author has been very careful to point out God's absolute sovereign grace in the salvation of his chosen people, while insisting it is the equally absolute responsibility of all men everywhere to repent of sin. Most religious teaching today makes it easy for people to live in sin and yet believe they have a right to heaven when they die. Pastor Fortner reminds us it is not so.

I was impressed while reading this book at the many references to the Holy Scriptures. Again, it is common in our day, in many quarters, to ignore, 'Thus saith the Lord'. But how can one write of heaven and not hear what 'the LORD, the God of heaven' has said about it? Brother Don has not been guilty of this! He has been careful to show from the Scriptures how the Lord Jesus Christ is both the only way to heaven, and the fulness of heaven to his Bride. No blood, no salvation! No salvation, no heaven!

You will find in the following pages not merely a series of chapters on the subject of heaven, which doubtless would be useful enough. It is certainly a superb exposition on the subject of heaven, and how God saves sinners in preparation for it. But you will find the book deals, too, with all aspects of a believer's attitude towards death, the confident assurance of joy to come, and many helpful scriptural comforts for the experience of dying.

I look forward to obtaining a finished copy of *Going Home* for my own benefit and recommend everyone purchase a copy and read it for themselves. I believe this book will prove to be very instructive for ministers of the gospel, and those involved pastorally with the Lord's people. It will be most helpful, too, to God's saints who live with eager expectation in hope of eternal life with God our Saviour in our heavenly home. Oh, the glory that awaits all of God's blood-bought children!

Earnie W. Lucas
Appomattox, Virginia

For the LORD God is a sun and shield: the LORD will give grace and glory: no good thing will he withhold from them that walk uprightly.

Psalm 84:11

Chapter 1

Grace And Glory

What is heaven? Do God's saints go to heaven immediately when they leave this world? What is the condition, or state, of the saints' existence in heaven? Who shall enter into heaven's glory? Upon what grounds do the saints enter into heaven?

These are the questions I hope to answer in this and the chapters that follow. I realize at the outset I can do no more than scratch the surface of this great subject. The glory awaiting God's saints in heaven, the vastness of our inheritance with Christ, is light years beyond the scope of our puny brains. I have no hope of exhausting this subject. In preparing these studies, I have purposefully avoided all matters of vain curiosity and speculation. It is my purpose to set forth some of those things which are plainly taught in the Word of God about the glorious state of God's saints in heaven.

Going Home

Psalm 84 is described in its title as 'A Marching Song' (see margin). In the eleventh verse, God's pilgrims are inspired in their march through this world with these words of promise: 'The Lord will give grace and glory.' The Psalmist takes our minds away from ourselves and calls our attention to 'The Lord' Jehovah, our God and Saviour. We must not look to ourselves in any measure for either grace here or glory hereafter. The Source of grace and glory is the Lord. The Security of grace and glory is God our Saviour. Christ alone is the Rock of our salvation. To him alone we must look for grace and glory.

Give
'The Lord will give grace and glory.' The word 'give' declares that neither grace nor glory can be earned, merited, or purchased by man in any way. This text, like all the Word of God, puts us upon the footing of grace. God cannot be obliged by man to bestow his grace; and he cannot be obliged by man to bestow glory. Both grace and glory are free gifts of God; and where he gives one he is sure to give the other.

Grace and glory are inseparable gifts. They are really the same thing. Grace is glory in the seed. Glory is grace in full bloom. Glory begins in grace and grace is completed in glory. Someone once said,

Grace is glory begun, and glory is grace consummated. Grace is glory in the bud, and glory is grace in the fruits. Grace is the lowest degree of glory, and glory is the highest degree of grace.

Grace And Glory

Grace and glory are two great and marvellous gifts which God bestows upon fallen men in Christ. The first thing he gives is grace. The last thing he gives is glory.

Grace

'The Lord will give grace.' How we love that word 'grace'. Grace is God's riches at Christ's expense. In the life, experience and hope of the believer everything is of grace, from the beginning to the end. Every believer gladly confesses, 'By the grace of God I am what I am.' The hymn writer Robert Robinson wrote,

> Oh, to grace how great a debtor
> Daily I'm constrained to be!
> Let that grace, Lord, like a fetter,
> Bind my wandering heart to Thee.

Read this promise in the boldest letters imaginable and rejoice. 'The Lord will give grace'! The promise comes from God the Lord. The Lord God Almighty, the great Jehovah, the triune God will most certainly, by his own irresistible power, according to his own sovereign will, give grace, freely and irreversibly.

To whom will the Lord give grace? We know he will give grace. The Word of God tells us so. It is asserted plainly. Someone is going to get grace from God. But who will it be?

The Lord will give grace to his own elect (Romans 9:15, 16). Grace belongs to God. It is his sovereign prerogative to give it to whom he will. And there are some among the fallen sons of men whom God has chosen to be the recipients of his grace (John 15:16; Matthew 11:25-27). Not one of those chosen in electing love, before the foundation of the world, to be a vessel of mercy shall fail to receive that grace before passing out of this world.

The Lord will give grace to every sinner redeemed by Christ's precious blood. Every sinner redeemed and purchased by Christ is his own possession and shall obtain grace. Christ did not die in vain! All whom he redeemed by blood shall have the grace of forgiveness (Ephesians 1:7; Colossians 1:14). All whom he purchased shall have the grace of reconciliation (Colossians 1:20). All for whom Christ was made a curse shall have the grace of free justification (Romans 8:34; Galatians 3:13). All for whom Christ was made sin shall have the grace of righteousness (2 Corinthians 5:21). All for whom he died shall have the grace of eternal life (John 10:8, 27).

The redemption Christ accomplished is an effectual redemption, and infallibly secures grace for all his redeemed ones. Not one of those whom Christ has redeemed from among men shall perish. Not one of his blood-bought sheep will be lost. Not one member of his body will be ruined. Not one part of his bride, the church, will be destroyed. Those whom Christ has redeemed will most assuredly obtain grace (Ephesians 5:25-27; John 10:16).[1]

The Lord will give grace to every believing sinner. We do not know who God's elect are, or who Christ has redeemed, except as they believe the gospel. Yet, we are assured by God himself that every believer is both elect and redeemed, because God promises grace to all who believe (Mark 16:16; John 1:12, 13; 3:14, 15, 36; Romans 10:9-13).

The long and short of the gospel is this: if you believe on the Lord Jesus Christ, if you trust his precious blood alone for your

---

[1] God's sovereign election and Christ's effectual redemption inspire us to preach the gospel fervently to every creature because we know 'the Lord will give grace' to his chosen, blood-bought people (Isaiah 53:9-11).

salvation and eternal acceptance with God, he will give you grace. I know a sinner cannot believe unless he has grace. But I also know you cannot have grace unless you believe. To every believing sinner it is promised, 'The Lord will give grace.'

What is this grace God promises to give? The psalmist does not say, 'The Lord will give some grace', 'graces', or 'a grace'. He declares, 'The Lord will give grace.' The implication is clear, wherever the Lord gives any grace, he gives all grace. 'The Lord will give ...

Regenerating Grace (Ephesians 2:1-5).
Justifying Grace (Romans 5:1-9).
Sanctifying Grace (Hebrews 10:10-14).
Preserving Grace (Philippians 1:6).
Instructing Grace (John 16:13).
Directing Grace (Proverbs 3:5, 6).
Comforting Grace (John 16:7; Lamentations 3:24, 25).
Reviving Grace (Isaiah 57:15).
Sufficient Grace (2 Corinthians 12:9).

How does the Lord give us his grace? God gives his grace to sinners mediatorially, through Christ our Mediator, through the use of the means he has ordained. Without question, God's saving grace comes to chosen sinners before they seek it (Isaiah 65:1). Yet, those who are sought of God are caused by grace to seek him; and he promises all who earnestly seek him shall find him (Jeremiah 29:13, 14). Believers are people who seek the Lord and seek his grace in Christ continually. He gives grace to those who seek it by prayer, through his Word, and in the keeping of his ordinances. These are the means by which God's grace is constantly bestowed upon his saints in this world. Furthermore, God gives us his grace seasonably. As our days demand, his grace is given. The Lord our God gives us his grace readily. He is always ready to be gracious. And the Lord our God gives us his grace constantly. Annie Johnson Flint wrote,

> He giveth more grace when the burdens grow greater,
> He sendeth more strength when the labours increase;
> To added affliction He addeth His mercy,
> To multiplied trials His multiplied peace.

Read this promise as broadly as you will. It is to you, child of God, in every condition and circumstance of life, 'The Lord will give grace'. He will give you grace to serve him (2 Corinthians 12:9), to suffer for him (Philippians 4:13), to endure temptations (1 Corinthians 10:13), and to die in him (2 Timothy 4:6-8).

Who is it will give grace? 'The Lord will give grace'! Grace is the gift of God alone. You will not get grace from yourself, from the church, from some imaginary priest, at some imaginary altar, or from the law of God. If we would get grace we must get it from God and only from God. The only way God gives grace is through Christ (John 1:16, 17). Look to Christ. Trust Christ. Believe Christ. Cling to Christ. As we do so, 'The Lord will give grace'! Again, the hymn writer wrote:

> In every condition, in sickness, in health;
> In poverty's vale, or abounding in wealth;
> At home and abroad, on the land, on the sea,
> As thy days may demand, shall thy strength ever be.

Glory

The Lord will give glory, too. The promise reads, 'The Lord will give grace and glory.' That little connecting word 'and' is more precious than gold. It is an indestructible rivet, forever uniting grace and glory. There are many who seem determined to take the rivet out; but they cannot. The text does not say, 'The Lord will give grace and perdition' or 'grace and purgatory' but 'The Lord will give grace and glory.' Nor does the text promise glory without grace. You can no more have glory without grace than you can have grace without glory. The two are joined, inextricably linked together. And what God has joined together let no man put asunder.

If we have grace, we shall have glory, too. God will not give one without the other. Grace, remember, is but the bud. Glory is the flower. Grace is the fountain. Glory is the river. Grace is the firstfruit. Glory is the full harvest. If we have grace, we shall never perish. We shall have glory. But those who do not have grace here shall never have glory hereafter. It is not possible for any to be glorified who have not first been justified. You cannot reign with Christ in glory if Christ does not reign in you by grace. Grace and glory are inseparable gifts of God. 'The Lord will give grace and glory.'

What is the glory he shall give? I am fully aware no puny, earthly brain can comprehend it (1 Corinthians 2:9). But God has revealed something of the glory awaiting us so our hearts may be drawn to it (1 Corinthians 2:10).

The glory we are to receive is the glory of heaven. And having said that, I have said more than I comprehend. Whatever heaven is, God will give it. It is a place of indescribable beauty. It is a state of indescribable bliss. Whatever may be meant by the figurative language that describes it,[2] all of heaven will be ours forever. The Lord will give the perfection of glory without measure to all to whom he has given grace without measure. You and I who trust Christ shall sit down with Abraham, Isaac, and Jacob at the throne of Christ the Lamb in the kingdom of God.

The glory God will give is the glory of eternity. Eternity! Who can define it? No one on earth can fathom the meaning of the word 'eternity'. We always confound eternity with time. We speak of the 'endless ages of eternity'. But there are no ages in eternity. Eternity will never pause, decline, or draw near to a conclusion. We will never grow weary of eternity. We will never grow weary in eternity. Eternity is unchanging, unending bliss.

Moreover, the glory God will give to his saints is the glory of Christ, our Mediator, Surety, and Covenant Head (Romans 8:17; John 17:22). Whatever the glory is that Christ has as our Mediator, as the reward for his perfect obedience to the Father, we shall have when we see him as he is in heaven. My heart pants to know, by actual experience the meaning of what I have just written. Oh, to know the glory waiting for us! Now we look through a glass darkly. We long to see him face to face, to have the clouds of darkness swept away, and to know and enter into his glory! In the serene atmosphere of heaven, we shall not only see the King in his beauty, but also possess his glory!

This glory will be the glory of total victory. We are more than conquerors through Christ our Lord (Romans 8:32-39). By the grace of God and the blood of the Lamb, we shall yet be victorious over the

---

[2] The streets of pure gold, the gates of pearl, the walls of jasper, the crowns, the palms, the harps, the songs, the river of the water of life, the trees bearing fruit, the tree of life. All that these things describe and all that heaven is the Lord God will give to his elect.

world, the flesh, and the devil (Romans 16:20). Death shall do us no harm, sin shall bring us no more grief, Satan shall tempt us no more, when the Lord gives us glory.

The glory the Lord will give us is the glory of a perfect nature (Ephesians 5:25-27; Jude 24, 25). This was and is the purpose and goal of God in predestination, election, redemption, and regeneration. God's work will not fail to accomplish his purpose. In heaven we shall have a perfect nature; spotless, sinless, and incorruptible. We shall have bodies without weakness, sickness, decay, or death. We shall have souls incapable of temptation, free from sin, care, and trouble. Our hearts shall be free of unbelief, sorrow, and pain. Our wills shall be in complete harmony with God's will. Imagine it! In glory we shall possess perfect natures! Holiness, absolute, perfect holiness shall be ours!

The glory promised to every believing sinner is the glory of perfect rest (Hebrews 4:11). Heaven's glory shall be a perpetual sabbath, an endless day of perfect peace, perfect happiness, perfect security. Charles H. Spurgeon said, 'It shall not be possible for a man to have a wish ungratified, nor a desire unfulfilled ... Every power shall find ample employment without weariness. And every passion shall have full indulgence, without so much as a fear of sin.' This is rest! This is glory! We shall want what our Saviour wants, do what our Saviour wills, love what our Saviour loves, and live for our Saviour's glory perfectly.

This glory is a gift of God's rich, free, abundant grace in Christ. 'The Lord will give grace and glory.' There is not a soul in heaven came there by his own merit. There is not a crown in heaven earned by the works of men. There is not a note of self-righteousness to mar the song of the redeemed. Glory is the gift of God.

When will the Lord give us this glory? Some will receive glory very soon. For some it will, perhaps, be a while yet. But of this we

21

can be sure absolutely, 'The Lord will give glory' as soon as our work here is done, no sooner and no later. And 'the Lord will give glory' at the hour he has purposed from eternity, no sooner and no later. Let us ever comfort one another with these words, 'The Lord will give grace and glory.' Our trials and troubles here are not worthy to be compared with the glory that awaits us (Romans 8:18).

Grace And Glory

The atoning work is done,
The Victim's blood is shed;
And Jesus now is gone
His people's cause to plead:
He stands in Heaven their great High Priest,
And bears their names upon His breast.

He sprinkles with His blood
The mercy-seat above;
For justice had withstood
The purposes of love:
But justice now objects no more,
And mercy yields her boundless store.

No temple made with hands
His place of service is;
In Heaven itself He stands,
A heavenly priesthood His:
In Him the shadows of the law
Are all fulfilled, and now withdraw.

And though awhile He be
Hid from the eyes of men,
His people look to see
Their great High Priest again:
In brightest glory He will come,
And take His waiting people home.

Thomas Kelly

Going Home

So I returned, and considered all the oppressions that are done under the sun: and behold the tears of such as were oppressed, and they had no comforter; and on the side of their oppressors there was power; but they had no comforter. Wherefore I praised the dead which are already dead more than the living which are yet alive.

Ecclesiastes 4:1, 2

Chapter 2

Where Have They Gone?
What Are They Doing?

The wise man, Solomon, after considering 'all the oppressions that are done under the sun', the tears of the oppressed in this world, the power of those who oppress, and the fact there is no comfort for God's saints in this world, said, 'I praised the dead which are already dead more than the living which are yet alive.' In the Book of Revelation, we read a similar statement, 'Blessed are the dead which die in the Lord' (14:13). Yet, when you and I go to the funeral home and graveside to bid our loved ones good-bye, we are filled with sorrow and weeping.

Why is it so? If the one God has taken is an unbeliever, the sorrow is understandable. Those who die in unbelief and sin die under the wrath of God. If our sorrow is the sorrow of parting friends, it is reasonable. None of us likes to part with cherished friends and loved ones, even temporarily. However, if the sorrow is the sorrow of those who have no hope, uncontrollable anguish, or even anger at God for having taken someone we love, I cannot understand that. Such sorrow reveals both ignorance and unbelief, ignorance of the blessed state of God's saints in heaven and unbelief regarding the Word of God, the promises of the gospel, and the finished work of Christ.

In this chapter, I want to show from the Scriptures that God's saints in heaven, our departed friends, are alive and well. Though their bodies have died and lay in the earth, they are more alive than ever and full of happiness.

Immediate Glory
First, let me show you from the Word of God how the souls of redeemed sinners, immediately after death, enter into heaven and into a state of eternal happiness. It is not my intention to answer the foolish questions of infidels, and heretics. Neither will we be side-tracked by the foolish speculations of ignorant men and women about life after death. As we think about the wonders of immortality, our only source of information is the Word of God. Only the eternal God can unveil the mysteries of eternity.

We are creatures of God made with immortal, undying souls. Though these bodies must die and rot in the earth like the brute beasts, our souls will exist forever. As soon as you die your soul will enter into a state of endless happiness or misery. Man does not die like a dog. When your dog dies, it is all there is to it. It ceases to be. But when you die, it is not all there is to it. Your soul lives on, not in a state of sleep, insensitivity, and inactivity, but in the fulness of life and consciousness.

The souls of believers, redeemed sinners, men and women who have been made righteous before God by the righteousness of Christ imputed to them, the souls of God's saints, return to God at death. Our departed brothers and sisters, as soon as they closed their eyes in death, opened them again in glory. There they will remain until the second coming of Christ. Then, when Christ comes again in his glory, he will bring them all with him, raise their bodies from the dust, and reunite their bodies and souls in resurrection glory. Believers yet living when Christ comes shall then be changed, glorified, caught up into glory. Thereafter, we shall forever be with the Lord (1 Thessalonians 4:13-18).

Though hell is as real as heaven and damnation as real as salvation, lest I turn your thoughts to matters of great sorrow and grief, I will say little about the horrible state of the wicked and unbelieving after death. They shall immediately, as soon as they close their eyes in death, wake up in the torments of hell. If the reader is yet without life, without faith, without Christ, and thus without hope, let him be warned. The wrath of God is upon you. If you die without Christ, you must be forever damned! To die without Christ is to die without hope. But for the believer things are different. The believer, as soon as he dies, is alive forever. His soul goes immediately home to God in heaven.

The Word of God, when speaking of the believer's death, always represents it as an immediate entrance into heavenly blessedness and glory. Actually, for the believer, death is not death at all, but the beginning of life. Our Lord said, 'Whosoever liveth and believeth in me shall never die' (John 11:26). God's elect never die. The death of the body is the liberty of the soul. And as soon as our souls are freed from this body of sin and death, we shall enter heaven.

When the righteous perish from the earth, they live in uprightness forever (Isaiah 57:1, 2). When the righteous die, they are taken away from evil, enter into a world of peace, and rest in their Saviour. Their bodies rest in hope in the grave, in hope of the resurrection. Their souls rest in the arms of Christ their Redeemer. Our departed friends have entered into everlasting rest (Hebrews 4:9-

11). There they walk in their uprightness. God reckons the righteousness of Christ imputed to us to be our righteousness here on earth. And he makes it ours perfectly and experimentally in heaven. There our departed brethren walk in their uprightness, in spotless purity and holiness, in shining robes of bliss and glory.

When a believer dies, he is carried by God's angels into heaven, Abraham's bosom, the place of endless comfort (Luke 16:22-25).[3]

Every believing sinner as soon as he dies is taken to be with Christ in paradise (Luke 23:43). Paradise is heaven, the garden of God (Revelation 2:7). It is the third heaven to which Paul was raptured for a brief visit during his pilgrimage here (2 Corinthians 12:2-4). Paradise is the place of the divine Majesty, the place of happiness, pleasure, and endless delight. It was to paradise Christ went as soon as he died, having obtained eternal redemption for us (Hebrews 9:12). Paradise is a place of assured blessedness, promised to sinners who seek the mercy of God in Christ. The dying Saviour said to the dying thief, who had just been converted by his omnipotent grace, 'Today (immediately, as soon as this ordeal of death is over) shalt thou (most assuredly) be with me (in my full presence and company forever) in paradise (heaven).'

Immeasurable Gain
Death for the believer is gain; infinite, immeasurable gain (Philippians 1:21, 23). Paul was confident that as soon as he departed from this world he would be immediately with Christ in blessed communion. Therefore, believing the Word and promise of God, he looked upon death as a desirable thing.

---

[3] 'Abraham's bosom' was a Jewish expression referring to the place of heavenly happiness prepared for God's saints between death and the resurrection.

What is the state of the saints' life between death and the resurrection? I will not say more than the Bible says. But this much I know, the souls of God's saints are not floating around in the sky. They have gone to a specific place where Christ is. They are assembled as a glorified church (Hebrews 12:22, 23). Their souls exist in a recognizable form. Moses and Elijah stood upon the mount of transfiguration in a recognizable form (Matthew 17:3). When the rich man saw Lazarus in Abraham's bosom, he saw and recognized him as the very same man who had lain by his gate upon the earth (Luke 16:23).

Do God's saints in heaven have a body between death and the resurrection? A physical body? No. A spiritual body, a heavenly form, a house for their souls? Most definitely (2 Corinthians 5:1). Every believer, as soon as he leaves this body, enters into heavenly glory with a heavenly body with Christ. It is this assurance of heavenly glory and bliss that makes death a desirable thing for the believer.

Welcome Relief
Second, we should always remember that for the believer the death of his body and the freeing of his soul is a welcome relief (Philippians 1:21-23; Revelation 14:13). While living in this world, we seek to be content with God's wise and good providence. We want to glorify our great God by living before him in faith, resigning all things to his will. We would not change our lot in life even if we could. Our heavenly Father knows and always does what is best.

Yet, life in this world is, at best, a burden to the heaven-born soul. In this tabernacle we groan (2 Corinthians 5:1-4). We groan for life! Our hearts cry, 'O wretched man that I am! Who shall deliver me from this body of death?' In this body we struggle with sin. In heaven we shall be free from sin. In this body we are tempted and often fall. In heaven we shall never be tempted and shall never fall. In this body we weep much. In heaven we shall weep no more. In this body we long to be like Christ. In heaven we shall be like Christ. In this body we long for Christ's presence. In heaven we shall forever be with Christ.

We have many friends in heaven whom we dearly love. We miss them. But we do not sorrow for them. We envy them! The believer, as long as he is in this world, is like an eagle I once saw while visiting a zoo in a foreign country. He sat on an iron perch, with a chain holding him to the earth, gazing into heaven. It appeared to me that he longed to soar away into the distant clouds; but the chain held him fast to the earth.

When an eagle is happy in an iron cage or chained to an iron perch, when a sheep is happy among a pack of wolves and a fish is happy on dry land, then, and not until then, will the renewed soul be happy in this body of flesh. Death for God's saints will be a welcome relief (Psalm 17:15).

Where?

We have seen from the Scriptures how God's saints, as soon as they die, enter into heaven, and death for the believer is a welcome relief. Now let me answer this question. Where have our departed friends gone? I have already shown you they have gone to heaven. They have not gone to purgatory. They are not in limbo. They are not floating around in the air. Their souls are not asleep. Our friends who have left us are in heaven. But where is heaven? That is a question I cannot answer. God has not told us. Heaven is a place somewhere outside of this world, somewhere outside of time. But it is a place, a real place, nevertheless. Heaven is the place where Christ is. Heaven is the place to which he has promised to bring us (John 14:1-3). Heaven is the place where our departed friends are right now (Hebrews 12:22, 23). Let us read 2 Corinthians 5:1-8.

> For we know that if our earthly house of this tabernacle were dissolved, we have a building of God, an house not made with hands, eternal in the heavens. For in this we groan, earnestly desiring to be clothed upon with our house which is from heaven: If so be that being clothed we shall not be found naked. For we that are in this tabernacle do groan, being burdened: not for that we would be unclothed, but clothed upon, that mortality might be swallowed up of life. Now he that hath wrought us for the selfsame thing is God, who also hath given unto us the earnest of the Spirit. Therefore we are always confident, knowing that, whilst we are at home in the body, we are absent from the Lord: (For we walk by faith, not by sight:) We are confident, I say, and willing rather to be absent from the body, and to be present with the Lord.

In these eight verses Paul tells us several things about the believer's death and entrance into heaven. Death is the dissolving of this earthly body. This body is of the earth. It is only suitable for the earth. It must return to the earth. And the dissolution of this body is no cause for sorrow. Richard Baxter wrote, 'It will be like taking off a shoe that hurts my foot – a welcome relief! It will be like laying aside a tool that is no longer needed because its work is done.' It will be like tearing down a tent to move into a house.

In heaven we shall have another house for our souls. 'In my Father's house are many mansions', houses, dwelling places. Whatever our house in heaven shall be, it shall be a house not made with hands, a house prepared by Christ, and a house suitable to our life in glory.

As soon as this earthly tabernacle is dissolved, we shall enter the house Christ has prepared for our souls in heaven. There will be no lapse of time, no delay, between the dissolving of this body and our entrance into our house in glory. This is not a matter of conjecture, but of certainty. 'We know', Paul says. We who are taught of God know these things by the revelation of God in his Word, by the earnest of the Spirit (v. 5), and by virtue of our faith in Christ (v. 7). What happens to the believer after death? Do you ask, 'Where have our departed friends gone?' They have gone to heaven. They have gone home. They have gone to be with Christ!

Heavenly Activity

One more question needs to be answered. What are God's saints doing in heaven? The Scriptures speak sparingly with regard to the saints' employment in heaven. But some things are revealed.

God's saints in heaven are celebrating and adoring the perfections of God in Christ (Revelation 5:11, 12; 7:11, 12). There they who behold his face speak with unceasing astonishment of his holiness, power, wisdom, goodness, grace, faithfulness, and love.

God's saints in heaven are delightfully employed in beholding the glory of God in the face of Christ (John 17:24). Oh, my soul, what will it be to behold the glory of our Redeemer? We shall forever behold him as he is, with a constantly increasing knowledge of him. Heaven is the Garden of God where the Rose of Sharon is in full bloom; and the fragrance of it perfumes the whole place. Heaven is to behold Christ forever, never taking our eyes off him, and never wanting to.

God's saints in heaven are employed in the constant exercise of every spiritual grace. The saints in heaven believe God. There our brethren patiently wait in hope of the resurrection. And they truly love one another.

God's saints in heaven are employed in the unending service of God (Revelation 7:14, 15). They are engaged in prayer (Revelation 6:10). They sing the songs of grace to the praise of God. Electing, redeeming, regenerating, justifying, sanctifying, preserving grace is the constant theme of their song around the throne of God.

God's saints in heaven are engaged in constant, uninterrupted fellowship with one another and with the holy angels. A casual reading of the book of Revelation conveys the idea that God's saints will forever discuss with one another and with the heavenly angels the wonders of covenant mercy, the ministry of the angelic hosts, redeeming love, saving grace, and divine providence.

Make certain you are in Christ. Let every child of God take comfort with regard to those who have gone to heaven. 'Blessed are the dead which die in the Lord'! And be assured, weary pilgrim, your weary, troublesome life will end soon and it will end well.

> For our light affliction, which is but for a moment, worketh for us a far more exceeding and eternal weight of glory; While we look not at the things which are seen, but at the things which are not seen: for the things which are seen are temporal; but the things which are not seen are eternal. For we know that if our earthly house of this tabernacle were dissolved, we have a building of God, an house not made with hands, eternal in the heavens. For in this we groan, earnestly desiring to be clothed upon with our house which is from heaven.
>
> 2 Corinthians 4:17-5:2

Going Home

To whom God would make known what is the riches of the glory of this mystery among the Gentiles; which is Christ in you, the hope of glory.

Colossians 1:27

Chapter 3

'The Hope Of Glory'

The gospel of God's free and sovereign grace in Christ is a mystery hidden from the unregenerate man, hidden from every unbeliever, but revealed by his Spirit to his saints, 'To whom God would make known what is the riches of the glory of this mystery among the Gentiles; which is Christ in you, the hope of glory.' There are three things revealed in this text.

The Riches Of Glory
First, all the riches promised, proclaimed, and presented to sinners in the gospel are in Christ. The riches of the gospel are spiritual riches. They are called, 'the riches of the glory of this mystery', because the glory of the gospel is, in great measure, to be seen in the riches of grace it holds in store for sinners who trust Christ.

What are these riches? They are the rich truths of grace, compared to gold, silver, and precious stones, by which God builds his holy temple (1 Corinthians 3:11-16). They are the rich truths of the gospel; sovereign election, substitutionary redemption, almighty, irresistible, saving grace, and the infallible preservation of God's saints in grace. The riches Paul speaks of are the rich treasures of grace laid up for sinners in Christ. In Christ there are immense and infinite treasures of grace laid up in store for God's elect (John 1:16; Ephesians 1:3; Colossians 2:9, 10). All the promises of God, relating to this life and to the life to come, are in Christ yea and amen, sure and infallible. In Christ we have free justification (Romans 3:24-26), absolute pardon (Ephesians 1:7), complete reconciliation (2 Corinthians 5:17), eternal adoption (1 John 3:1, 2), and eternal life (Romans 3:23).

The Glory Of The Gospel
Second, Christ is also the glory of the gospel. Read Colossians 1:27 again. 'To whom God would make known what is the riches of the glory of this mystery among the Gentiles; which is Christ.' The gospel is the revelation of the glory of God; and the glory of God is Christ. We see the glory of God in the face of Jesus Christ. That is to say, by faith in Christ every believer sees what was revealed to Moses in Exodus 34. They see God's glorious, sovereign goodness and his inflexible justice in the exercise of his saving grace in Christ (Isaiah 45:20). God's glory is known and revealed only in the Lord Jesus Christ, the incarnate God, and the sinner's Substitute (John 1:18; 17:3; 2 Corinthians 4:6).

The Hope Of Glory
Third, the believer's hope of glory is Christ. 'Christ in you, the hope of glory.' We live in hope of immortality and eternal life in heavenly glory. The basis, foundation, and ground of our hope is, 'Christ in you, the hope of glory.' That is the subject of this chapter. The glory which the saints will have with Christ will be the enjoyment of him forever in heaven. This hope of glory in which we live is brought to light by the gospel. As John Gill said concerning Christ our hope of glory:

'The Hope Of Glory'

Glory itself is in his hands. The gift of it is with him and through him. He has made way by his sufferings and death for the enjoyment of it, and is now preparing it for us by his presence and intercession. His grace makes us worthy of it. His righteousness gives us title to it. And his Spirit is the earnest of it.

The hope of glory which we have in Christ is built solely upon Christ himself. It is a hope founded on his blood, righteousness, intercession, and grace. Here are ten facts revealed in the Scriptures which assure us that our hope of glory is a good, well-grounded, and sure hope. We hope to go to heaven when we die. But more, we hope for immortality and eternal life in glory with Christ because of ...

1. What God Has Promised

God has promised eternal life and glory to his elect. It is written, 'The Lord will give grace and glory' (Psalm 84:11). God promises to godly men and women not only spiritual life that now is, but also eternal life which is to come (1 Timothy 4:8). This promise of eternal life, life with Christ forever in glory, is the principal, all-encompassing promise of the gospel. It is the centre of all the promises of God. Indeed, all other blessings of grace terminate in this. 'This is the promise that he promised us, even eternal life' (1 John 2:25). It is a promise made by God, who cannot lie, before the world began (Titus 1:2). This is a promise to be depended upon. It is sure and certain. When this life is over God's saints will enter into eternal life in glory. 'Blessed is the man that endureth temptation: for when he is tried', when he has been proved by the trials and afflictions of life in this world, 'he shall receive the crown of life, which the Lord hath promised to them that love him' (James 1:12). And the crown of life is the 'crown of glory that fadeth not away' (1 Peter 5:4).

2. What God Has Prepared

The glory of eternal life in heaven is a glory God has prepared for his elect. It is a glory unseen, unheard of, and inconceivable to the minds of men and women in this world. But it is a glory prepared by God for them that love him (1 Corinthians 2:9). This preparation of eternal happiness was made for us before the world began.

Heaven is a kingdom prepared for God's elect from the foundation of the world (Matthew 25:34). It was prepared in the counsels and purposes of God, which cannot be defeated, frustrated, or made void by any means. And this kingdom of glory shall, most assuredly, be given to those men and women for whom it was prepared by God (Matthew 20:23). It will not be given to any but those for whom it was prepared. It cannot be purchased, earned, won, or in any way merited by the works of men. But it shall be given freely to those for whom God prepared it.

3. God's Will For His People

God's elect in this world are men and women he has prepared unto glory (Romans 9:23). Not only has God promised and prepared a kingdom of glory for his elect, but his elect are 'vessels of mercy which he had afore prepared unto glory'. Every work of God's grace is a preparatory work whereby he prepares his people to enter into and enjoy everlasting glory.

God prepared us unto glory in sovereign predestination, having ordained us to eternal life. At God's appointed 'time of love' (Ezekiel 16:8), those who were ordained to eternal life are given grace to believe on the Lord Jesus Christ and effectually caused to come to him in faith by the Spirit of grace (Acts 13:48; Psalm 65:4).

Those whom God has ordained to eternal life and caused to believe on Christ shall most assuredly enjoy that life in eternity to which they were ordained from eternity. The means of bringing God's elect into eternal life in glory as well as eternal life itself has been infallibly fixed by God's decree (2 Thessalonians 2:13, 14).

'God hath from the beginning chosen you to salvation', not from the beginning of your repentance, faith, and conversion, but from the beginning of time, from eternity. All who now believe, and all who ever shall believe were chosen by God to salvation before the world began.

The means by which God determined to save us is plainly revealed. 'Through sanctification of the Spirit' that is, our regeneration. 'And belief of the truth' that is our faith in Christ. 'Whereunto he called you by our gospel' that is the preaching of the gospel.

That salvation and eternal life to which we have been elected, predestinated, and called is eternal glory. 'To the obtaining of the glory of our Lord Jesus Christ.' We shall obtain that very same glory which Christ has entered into and now possesses. He has it in his hands to give to God's elect (John 17:2). He declares it to be ours (John 17:5, 20). We have been predestinated to it (Romans 8:29). And we shall have it (Romans 8:28-31). Nothing is able to prevent it.

Here is a marvellous, golden chain of grace not to be broken. It begins in predestination and ends in glorification. 'Whom he did predestinate, them he also called: and whom he called them he also justified: and whom he justified, them he also glorified'!

4. God's Eternal Decrees
The hope of glory arises from the covenant of grace ordered in all things and sure (2 Samuel 23:5). The covenant of grace includes among its many blessings an everlasting inheritance of happiness and

glory, and every believer may be assured of its possession (Ephesians 1:10-14). It is called a covenant of grace, because it arises from and is founded upon the pure, free grace of God in Christ and is filled with all the blessings of grace. In the Scriptures it is called the covenant of peace (Ezekiel 37:26), because it has for its end the restoration of sinners to God in peace and reconciliation by Christ (Malachi 2:5). It is called also the covenant of life for the same reason. It finds its full accomplishment in eternal life in glory.

It is a covenant ordered in all things and sure. Everything necessary for our spiritual and eternal welfare was provided and secured by our God in this covenant before the world was made (Ephesians 1:3-9). The blessings of the covenant are everything involved in our salvation. It comprehends and secures everything respecting our spiritual happiness in both this world and in the world to come.

This covenant of grace is all our desire. There is nothing good, nothing desirable for our soul's everlasting happiness and glory, that is not provided and secured in the covenant. The hope of glory in which we now live arises from the covenant of grace made between God the Father, God the Son, and God the Holy Spirit before the world began.

5. God's Covenant Is Not In Vain

The suretyship engagements and performances of Christ as our Covenant Head and Representative assure us our hope of glory is not vain.

All God promised and pledged to his elect in the covenant was made sure to us by Christ, the Surety of the covenant (Hebrews 7:22-25). Christ became a Surety for his people in the covenant of grace. As such, he pledged himself not only to bring the blessings of grace to us in time, but also to bring us to glory in eternity. He pledged not only that he would bring us to himself in faith and into the fold of his church upon earth, but also to set us before his Father's face in heaven (John 10:16).

As Judah became surety for Benjamin (Genesis 43:9), promising to bring him and set him before the face of his father, Jacob, or bear the blame forever, so Christ, the Lion of the tribe of Judah, became Surety for God's elect and promised to bring them, every one, to glory at last.

As our great Surety, Christ looked upon himself as being under obligation to do everything required by the law and justice and mercy and grace of God to bring us home to God in heaven. He became responsible to God for our everlasting salvation. Therefore, in the fulness of time, he came into the world to remove our sins, establish righteousness for us, and open before us the way to God. He came that we might have life and that we might have it more abundantly (John 10:10). He came to give us a more excellent and abundant life than Adam had in his innocence, or the angels have in heaven. He came to give us a life of glory with himself.

Christ our Surety is 'the hope of glory'. He is the Captain of our salvation. As such, he will bring many sons to glory and present them to the Father, saying, 'Behold, I and the children whom God hath given me' (Hebrews 2:10-13). This is what the Apostle means when he says, 'Wherefore he is able to save them to the uttermost that come to God by him'!

6. We Have A Forerunner
We are further assured or re-assured of the hope of glory by Christ's entrance into glory as our Forerunner (Hebrews 6:20).

After his resurrection from the dead, the Lord Jesus Christ ascended up into heaven and entered into glory, not for himself, but for us, as the Head and Representative of God's elect, for whom he had suffered, bled, and died upon the cursed tree. He entered into heaven as our Forerunner, took possession of it in our name, and now appears in the presence of God for us (Hebrews 9:24). Our Redeemer's representation of us in glory is so real a representation and so absolutely secures our entrance into glory with him that we are said to be already seated together with him in heavenly places (Ephesians 2:6).

7. The Prayers And Preparations Of Christ
The prayers and preparations of Christ for the future glory of his people assure us of the hope of glory. Our Saviour has gone to heaven to prepare a place for us (John 14:2). He says, 'In my Father's house are many mansions' abiding houses of wealth, places filled with peace, joy, and happiness. 'If it were not so, I would have told you.' If heavenly glory were nothing but a dream and vain delusion, I would have told you. I would not deceive you with a false hope. 'I go to prepare a place for you.'

Our all-glorious Saviour has gone to heaven, the Father's house, to prepare a place for us, his beloved friends. Yes, heavenly glory is a kingdom prepared for us from the foundation of the world by the purpose and decree of God. Yet, it required another, fresh preparation by the bodily presence, blood atonement, and gracious intercession of Christ. Christ is in heaven preparing a place for chosen sinners. This is his particular business in heaven. He is preparing a place for us!

One great part of that preparation is our Saviour's intercession to God on our behalf. Christ, our great High Priest, is making intercession to God on behalf of his elect, redeemed people. He is praying for the salvation of those who yet believe not (Hebrews 7:25), the non-imputation of sin to his erring people (1 John 2:1, 2), the spiritual unity of his church (John 17:21), the preservation of his elect (John 17:15), and the eternal happiness of his saints in heaven (John 17:24).

When our place in heaven is perfectly prepared for us and we for it, Christ will come to take us home to glory (John 14:3). 'If I go and prepare a place for you, I will come again, and receive you unto myself; that where I am, there ye may be also.' Sickness is the voice of our Beloved calling us home. Death is the car he sends to take us home. Our departed brothers and sisters in Christ, our friends and companions in the kingdom of God are already there, at home with Christ in the Father's house.

8. The Work Of The Holy Ghost

The hope of glory is born in our souls by the effectual call of God the Holy Spirit.

The apostle Paul admonished Timothy to 'lay hold on eternal life', to look for it, expect it, anticipate it, and believe that he would enter into it at last. The basis for his admonition was, 'whereunto thou art also called' (1 Timothy 6:12).

Like Timothy, every believer has been called to eternal life and glory in Christ. Therefore, we are exhorted to 'walk worthy of God, who hath called (us) unto his kingdom and glory' (1 Thessalonians 2:12). And we are assured 'the God of all grace, who hath called us unto his eternal glory by Christ Jesus' (1 Peter 5:10) will bring us safely home to glory at last. Those whom he has called, he will also glorify. We are called to glory. And we shall enter glory by the grace of God.

9. The Earnest Of The Spirit

The hope of glory which we have in Christ is a good and lively hope, because we have the earnest of the Spirit (2 Corinthians 5:5; Ephesians 1:14).

The Holy Spirit has been given to us in regeneration as the earnest, the down payment, the first instalment, of our inheritance in glory. We are sealed by him until the day of our full redemption and entrance into everlasting glory. As surely as God has given us his Spirit, the earnest of our inheritance, in regeneration, he will also give us the fulness of our inheritance in Christ in glorification. The Holy Spirit, and eternal life by his grace and power, is a well of living water in the hearts of God's saints springing up into everlasting life in glory (John 4:14).

10. God's Gift Of Assurance

The hope of glory which we have in Christ fills the believer's heart with desires for glory with Christ (Psalm 27:4).

In this tabernacle of flesh we groan, earnestly desiring to be clothed with the perfection of everlasting glory in the presence of Christ, that mortality might be swallowed up of life (2 Corinthians 5:1-4). As we begin to apprehend the glory that awaits us, we desire to depart and be with Christ, which is far better than anything we can experience in this world (Philippians 1:23). We choose rather to be absent from the body and to be present with the Lord than to go on in this weak and sinful frame of flesh (2 Corinthians 5:8).

Those who die in faith, die in happiness, knowing they are going to a city whose Builder and Maker is God (Hebrews 11:3). They are confident, with David, that as God has guided them in life with his counsel, he will at the end of life receive them up to glory (Psalm 73:24). 'For we know that if our earthly house of this tabernacle were dissolved, we have a building of God, an house not made with hands, eternal in the heavens' (2 Corinthians 5:1).

How many saints, and even martyrs, have cried, as they were about to leave this world, 'Glory! Glory! Glory!' as if they had seen it and were leaving this world to go to it. The infidels of this world think such men and women to be enthusiastic dreamers. But the believer looks with envy upon his departing friends, because we have within us the hope of glory to which they have already gone.

The believer's 'hope of glory' is a matter of unquestionable fact, plainly revealed in Holy Scripture. Believers, as soon as they depart from this world, are immediately with Christ in glory. Those who die in Christ are truly blessed of God, from the moment of their death and forever. 'The angels stand around their dying beds waiting to do their office; and as soon as the soul is separated from the body, escort it through the regions of the air to heavenly bliss' says John Gill. Lazarus, as soon as he died, was carried by the angels into Abraham's bosom (Luke 16:22). The penitent thief, on the day he died by Christ's side, was carried with Christ into paradise (Luke 23:43). Every believer who has died in faith is now in heaven. And you and I, if we are born of God, if we live by faith in Christ, as soon as we die, shall be with Christ in glory!

Going Home

Dearest Saviour, call us soon
To Thine high eternal noon;
Never there shall tempest rise,
To conceal Thee from our eyes:
Satan shall no more deceive,
We no more Thy Spirit grieve;
But through cloudless, endless days,
Sound, to golden harps, Thy praise.

John Newton

Revelation 21:1-27

And I saw a new heaven and a new earth: for the first heaven and the first earth were passed away; and there was no more sea. And I John saw the holy city, new Jerusalem, coming down from God out of heaven, prepared as a bride adorned for her husband. And I heard a great voice out of heaven saying, Behold, the tabernacle of God is with men, and he will dwell with them, and they shall be his people, and God himself shall be with them, and be their God. And God shall wipe away all tears from their eyes; and there shall be no more death, neither sorrow, nor crying, neither shall there be any more pain: for the former things are passed away. And he that sat upon the throne said, Behold, I make all things new. And he said unto me, Write: for these words are true and faithful. And he said unto me, It is done. I am Alpha and Omega, the beginning and the end. I will give unto him that is athirst of the fountain of the water of life freely. He that overcometh shall inherit all things; and I will be his God, and he shall be my son. But the fearful, and unbelieving, and the abominable, and murderers, and whoremongers, and sorcerers, and idolaters, and all liars, shall have their part in the lake which burneth with fire and brimstone: which is the second death.

And there came unto me one of the seven angels which had the seven vials full of the seven last plagues, and talked with me, saying, Come hither, I will shew thee the bride, the Lamb's wife. And he carried me away in the spirit to a great and high mountain, and shewed me that great city, the holy Jerusalem, descending out of heaven from God, Having the glory of God: and her light was like unto a stone most precious, even like a jasper stone, clear as crystal; And had a wall great and high, and had twelve gates, and at the gates twelve angels, and names written thereon, which are the names of the twelve tribes of the children of Israel: On the east three gates; on the north three gates; on the south three gates; and on the west three gates. And the wall of the city had twelve foundations, and in them the names of the twelve apostles of the Lamb. And he that talked with me had a golden reed to measure the city, and the gates thereof, and the wall thereof. And the city lieth foursquare, and the length is as large as the breadth: and he measured the city with the reed, twelve thousand furlongs. The length and the breadth and the height of it are equal. And he measured the wall thereof, an hundred and forty and four cubits, according to the measure of a man, that is, of the angel. And the building of the wall of it was of jasper: and the city was pure gold, like unto clear glass. And the foundations of the wall of the city were garnished with all manner of precious stones. The first foundation was jasper; the second, sapphire; the third, a chalcedony; the fourth, an emerald; The fifth, sardonyx; the sixth, sardius; the seventh, chrysolite; the eighth, beryl; the ninth, a topaz; the tenth, a chrysoprasus; the eleventh, a jacinth; the twelfth, an amethyst. And the twelve gates were twelve pearls; every several gate was of one pearl: and the street of the city was pure gold, as it were transparent glass. And I saw no temple therein: for the Lord God Almighty and the Lamb are the temple of it. And the city had no need of the sun, neither of the moon, to shine in it: for the glory of God did lighten it, and the Lamb is the light thereof. And the nations of them which are saved shall walk in the light of it: and the kings of the earth do bring their glory and honour into it. And the gates of it shall not be shut at all by day: for there shall be no night there. And they shall bring the glory and honour of the nations into it. And there shall in no wise enter into it any thing that defileth, neither whatsoever worketh abomination, or maketh a lie: but they which are written in the Lamb's book of life.

Chapter 4

Images Of Heavenly Glory

Please take the time to read Revelation chapter twenty-one. In that chapter the Holy Spirit gives us several biblical images representing the present and everlasting state of God's saints in heaven's glory. It is not my intention in this study to explain all the mysteries of that chapter. I know the impossibility of the task. We will never know the fulness of the glory awaiting us until we experience it. But the things recorded in those twenty-seven verses do give us some images of the heavenly glory awaiting every believer.

In this series of studies I am trying to describe the glorious state of God's saints in heaven, a task more fit for an angel than for a man, or for one of the glorified saints in heaven than for a weak, sinful, mortal creature like myself. But it is a task God has, I believe, laid upon my heart and one in which I thoroughly delight. Our conception of heavenly glory and the greatness of it must be formed according to the adjectives used in the Word of God to describe it.

Unseen Glory
It is an unseen glory (1 Corinthians 2:9). The glory of heaven consists of 'things not seen' (2 Corinthians 4:18) which are eternal. We look for and have an assured hope of heaven by faith. But no one on earth has ever seen it (1 Corinthians 2:9; Hebrews 11:1.) No one here has ever had so much as a glimpse of heaven but by faith. We live in hope of that which we have not yet seen (Romans 8:24, 25).

Future Glory
The glory of heaven is for us a future glory (Romans 8:18; 1 John 3:2). Our friends who have gone before us enjoy the glory of heaven now. But for us, it is altogether a future thing, yet to be revealed. Sometimes we imagine we have experienced a little foretaste of heaven, or a little of 'heaven on earth', in the worship of our God; but we have never come close. The glory of heaven is a glory yet to be revealed.

Incomparable Glory
It is also an incomparable glory (Romans 8:18). There is nothing in this world to be compared to the glory of heaven. All earthly honour, riches, pleasure, and greatness are trifling and empty things of vanity, when compared to the glory that awaits us. Even the sufferings of God's saints in this world for Christ's sake, which is the purest and most glorious form of service to him, is not worthy to be compared to the glory that awaits us. And if our most glorious services cannot be compared to the glory of heaven, they certainly cannot be meritorious of heaven! The very best things we do for our God, from the purest principles, cannot be compared to heavenly glory. Our afflictions for Christ are 'light afflictions'. Heaven is a weight of

glory. Our afflictions are 'but for a moment'. Heavenly glory is eternal.

The prospect of heavenly glory supports believers in their troubles. It makes them choose to suffer affliction with the people of God and to esteem the reproach of Christ greater riches than the treasures of Egypt. It causes them to take joyfully the spoiling of their goods for Christ's sake, knowing that in heaven they have a better and an enduring substance (Hebrews 11:25, 26; 10:34). If nothing in this world can be compared to the glory that awaits us in heaven, then let us set our hearts on things above, not on things on the earth (Colossians 3:1-4; Matthew 6:19-34).

My rest is in heaven, my rest is not here,
Then why should I tremble when trials come near?
Be hushed, my dark spirit, the worst that can come,
But shortens thy journey, and hastens thee home.

It is not for me to be seeking my bliss,
Or building my hopes in a region like this;
I look for a city that hands have not piled,
I pant for a country by sin undefiled.

The thorn and the thistle around us may grow,
We would not lie down, e'en on roses below:
We ask not our portion, we seek not a rest,
Till in glory for ever with Christ we are blest.

Afflictions oppress me, but cannot destroy,
One glimpse of His love turns them all into joy;
The bitterest tears, if He smiles but on them,
Like dew in the sunshine, turn diamond or gem.

Let doubt, then, and danger my progress oppose,
They only make heaven more sweet at the close,
Come joy, or come sorrow, whatever befall,
One hour with my God will make up for them all.

A scrip on my back, a staff in my hand,
I march on in haste through an enemy's land;
The road may be rough, but it cannot be long;
I'll smooth it with hope and cheer it with song.

Henry Francis Lyte (1793-1847)

Eternal Glory
The glory awaiting us in heaven is called an eternal glory (1 Peter 5:10). The glory of this world passes away very quickly. But the glory of the world to come never shall. The glory of this world is fading. The glory of that world is unending. The glory of this world is temporal. The glory of that world is everlasting. The glory of heaven is an immutable, eternal weight of glory. All that awaits us on the other side is eternal. It is ...

A crown of glory that fadeth not away.
An inheritance that is eternal.
A house, not made with hands, eternal in the heavens.
A kingdom that is everlasting.
A city that abides and continues forever.

John Gill tells us, 'when kingdoms, crowns, and sceptres are no more, and all that is great and glorious in this world (has passed away), this will endure forever, for it is eternal glory the God of all grace calls his people to and will put them in possession of.'

Here is the glory of heaven. It is to be forever with the Lord. It is eternity with Christ!

> This world is not my home,
> I'm only passing through;
> A stranger here, I must go on,
> My home is now in view:
> 'Forever with the Lord'!
> Amen! So let it be!
> With Christ I'll live forevermore
> In immortality!

A Place Of Glory

Add to all this the fact that heaven is a place of glory (John 14:3). Our Lord said, 'I go and prepare a place for you'. Yes, heaven is a state and condition of glory. But it is also a place of glory, a place to which Christ has gone, a place where he sits in a real body upon a glorious throne, a place prepared for us.

The glory of that place called heaven is set forth in the Scriptures under many striking images, images taken from the greatest, most glorious, richest and most valuable things known to men. We know that the imagery used in the Scriptures to describe heaven is not given to describe its literal form, size, and shape, because Paul told us plainly that no tongue could describe what he saw there and heard there (2 Corinthians 12:1-4). Those images drawn of heaven by the inspired writers of God's Word are intended to show us the surpassing excellence and infinite glory that awaits us in heaven.

Here are five images given in the Word of God to show us the grandeur and greatness of heavenly glory.

A House

Heaven is represented to us in the Scriptures as a house (2 Corinthians 5:1). It is a house, but a house incomparable to any house found in this world. This house is a building of God, 'a house not made with hands, eternal in the heavens'.

This house of glory is not built by man's hands. This is a house whose Builder and Maker is God. There is nothing, not one brick or piece of timber in that heavenly house that has been laid in its place by the will of man, the works of man, or the worship of man. Our house in heaven is a construction of grace alone. It is true, the works of God's saints follow them into their house in heaven (Revelation 14:13). But they do not go before them. Nor do they have anything to do with the building of that house. It is a building of God. Its foundation was laid in God's purpose. Its walls were erected by Christ's obedience. Its title deed was purchased by Christ's blood. Its door was opened by Christ's entrance into heaven.

Solomon built a great temple in Jerusalem. When it was laid in ruins, Zerubbabel rebuilt it, and Herod repaired it. It was a grand and glorious structure in the eyes of men. But where is it now? Not one stone is left in its place. It was a holy place made with hands. But it was only a temporary, typical house. Our house in heaven is the true holy place. It is the building of God, the work of free, sovereign, effectual grace in the Lord Jesus Christ.

This house is in the heavens (2 Corinthians 5:2). Our present houses of clay, the physical bodies in which we now live, have their foundation in the dust of the earth. Therefore, they must soon crumble. But our house which is from heaven and in heaven is eternal. It will never age, or crumble, or stand in need of repair. Men build their houses on earth and vainly imagine they will stand forever (Psalm 49:11). But in time they decay, are demolished by the elements, broken down through earthquakes, burned with fire, or destroyed by their enemies. Our heavenly house of glory abides forever. All its apartments are called 'everlasting habitations' (Luke 16:9).

Our Lord Jesus called this house our 'Father's house' (John 14:2). It is his Father's house. That makes it our Father's house, and that makes it all the more endearing and glorious. In our Father's house there are many mansions. Roll this morsel around in your heart. Heaven is called the 'Father's house'. Our Father built it. Our Father dwells there. It is the place where He would have all his children to be. Our Father's house is a rich, roomy, stately, and well stored house, a place of 'many mansions'. These mansions are dwelling places for the King's sons. They are places of rest, joy, and peace, where the sons and daughters of Almighty God want for nothing. And there are 'many' of them! 'Many' for the many who were ordained to eternal life. The many who have been justified by Christ's obedience. The many for whom his blood was shed for the remission of sins. And the many sons whom he will bring to glory (Acts 13:48; Romans 5:19; Matthew 26:28; Hebrews 2:10). There is room enough and provision enough in the Father's house for all the innumerable hosts of those men and women out of every nation, kindred, tribe and tongue who are chosen, redeemed, and called by almighty grace.

An Inheritance
Heavenly glory is called an inheritance (Acts 20:32; Ephesians 1:11; Colossians 1:12; Romans 8:17). As Canaan was an inheritance distributed by lot to the children of Israel, so heavenly glory is an inheritance given by lot, by the lot which God himself arranged

(Proverbs 16:33), to the Israel of God. Canaan is a type of heaven, and it should never be forgotten that Moses could never bring Israel into the land. But what Moses through the weakness of the flesh could not do, Joshua did. And the saints of God are brought to heaven not by the works of the law, but by the Lord Jesus Christ, our Joshua, our Deliverer, the Captain of our salvation.

An inheritance is a free gift. It cannot be earned by labour and diligence. It cannot be merited. It cannot be purchased with money. It is bequeathed from one person to another. Our inheritance in heavenly glory was given by God the Father to his Son, Christ Jesus our Lord. It is given by Christ to all who trust him. It is to us a gift of pure, free, sovereign grace. Be sure you understand these things.

Heavenly glory cannot be obtained, in any part or degree, by the works of men. All men by nature vainly imagine they must do something to inherit eternal life in heaven. But their proud imaginations deceive them. Eternal life is the gift of God (Romans 6:23) in its promise, in its bestowment, in its preservation, and in its everlasting enjoyment. Heavenly glory cannot be purchased by men. If a man should give all his substance for it, the price offered would be utterly despised by God. Heavenly glory is an inheritance bequeathed to chosen sinners by our heavenly Father from eternity. It is the Father's good pleasure to give his kingdom to his elect. He gives it by his own will, by a testament, through, by, and upon the merits of the sacrificial death of his dear Son, the Testator (Hebrews 9:15-17).

This inheritance belongs only to the children of God (Romans 8:17). It does not belong to his servants, the angels (Hebrews 1:14), nor to the children of the bond-woman (Galatians 4:30); the self-righteous, legalistic, work-mongers and free-will religionists still in slavery to sin. It belongs only to those men and women predestinated to adoption in eternity and called to be the sons of God in time. Yet, it is an inheritance that belongs to all the saints of God fully. There are no degrees of glory in heaven. There are no back settlements in the heavenly Canaan! There are no second class citizens in the New Jerusalem!

Our heavenly inheritance is incorruptible. All earthly inheritances are corruptible, subject to change, and unstable. This inheritance cannot be corrupted by us or anyone else. It cannot be changed or altered in any degree. It is as sure as the throne of God. It is an undefiled inheritance. It is an inheritance that fadeth not away. It is an eternal inheritance (Hebrews 9:15). It is an inheritance reserved in heaven, immutably and infallibly reserved in heaven for God's elect (1 Peter 1:4). God keeps the inheritance for us; and God keeps us for the inheritance.

A City
Another familiar image of heaven is that of a city (Hebrews 11:10). Heaven is a large, rich, spacious, fully inhabited city, whose Builder and Maker is God. Like the other images, this word 'city' is a figurative term, not to be understood in any carnal, earthly, mundane sense. Heaven is a city infinitely beyond anything on this earth.

It is 'a city which hath foundations'. Not one foundation, but many, so it is firm, immovable, and cannot be shaken, thrown down, or dissolved. The foundations upon which this city, this habitation of glory, is built are the everlasting love of God, the unalterable covenant of grace, and the blessed Rock of Ages, Jesus Christ our Lord.

The glory of this city cannot be comprehended or described by men upon this earth (2 Corinthians 12:4). The description of the New Jerusalem given by the Apostle John is a hyperbole. It does exactly what it was intended to do. It defies imagination. John saw in his vision a city with walls of jasper, gates of pearl, and streets of pure gold, transparent as glass! What a place of spiritual wealth, abundance, and happiness heaven must be! What a place of spiritual excellence and perfection! There in heaven there is no value, absolutely no value, for the most priceless treasures and gems of the world! In that world, where there is no sin, there is no greed, nor covetousness, nor ambition. In that glory land, where there is no sin, priceless material things are looked upon as nothing but useful accommodations. No value is placed upon them. Jasper is nothing but a wall to enclose the church of God. Pearls are nothing but gates to open the kingdom of God. Gold is nothing but pavement upon which men and women walk to the throne of God. May God graciously teach us so to use them now!

A Kingdom

Heavenly glory is represented to us as a kingdom. A mansion is great. An inheritance is something greater. A city is something greater still. But the inspired writers seem to stretch for words to describe the heavenly glory, using ever expanding ideas to describe it. What is heaven? It is a glorious house! Yes, but it is more than a house. It is a glorious inheritance! Yes, but it is more than an inheritance. It is a glorious city! Yes, but it is more than a city. It is a glorious kingdom!

God's saints in this world are kings. We have a kingdom now which cannot be moved (Hebrews 12:28). It is a kingdom that lies not in carnal ceremonies, but in righteousness, peace, and joy in the Holy Spirit (Romans 14:17). And we are heirs of another kingdom also, a kingdom prepared for us from the foundation of the world (Matthew 25:35). It is a kingdom of glory (1 Thessalonians 2:12). It is an everlasting kingdom. We have been called and born into this kingdom by the almighty, irresistible grace and power of God the Holy Spirit. We have been prepared and fitted for this kingdom by the blood and righteousness of Christ.

Images Of Heavenly Glory

The kingdom of glory to which we are heirs is the place where every believer shall be crowned and honoured by God and all the holy angels. In this world, among men, there is no honour put upon faith, faithfulness, and commitment to Christ. But in the world to come God himself and all his holy angels will honour and crown redeemed sinners for the perfection of beauty which grace has given them in Christ (Ephesians 1:10; 2:7; Revelation 21:9, see also Jeremiah 33:16). The Lord God himself will give us a crown: a crown of life (James 1:12), a crown of righteousness (2 Timothy 4:8), a crown of glory that fadeth not away (1 Corinthians 9:25).

Our great God and Saviour will cause us to sit upon a throne as kings in his glorious kingdom (Revelation 3:21). We have been raised from the dunghill of fallen humanity by his grace. And we shall be raised and lifted from the dunghill to a throne of glory in heaven (1 Samuel 2:8). There, in heavenly glory, we shall inherit and sit upon the throne with our ever blessed Lord Jesus Christ himself. This is grace! This is glory!

Eternal Pleasure
Heavenly glory is set before us under the image of infinite, eternal, holy pleasure (Psalm 16:11). Heaven is a house. Heaven is an inheritance. Heaven is a city. Heaven is a kingdom. And heaven is a place of glorious life, fulness of joy, and pleasure for ever more. Everything that is pleasing to the renewed mind, gratifying to the sanctified heart, and desirable to the regenerate soul shall be fully enjoyed to all eternity in heaven's glory land.

There we shall sit down with Christ at his table and drink new wine with him in his Father's kingdom. There we shall pick and eat the fruit of the Tree of Life which stands in the midst of the paradise of God. There we shall drink of that pure River of the Water of Life proceeding out of the throne of God and of the Lamb. There we shall see what no eye has seen, hear what no ear has heard, and understand that which has never before entered into the heart of man. John Gill again, says,

> The eye of man has seen many things on earth very grand and illustrious, and what have been very entertaining to it; but it never saw such objects as will be seen in heaven. The ear of man has heard and been entertained with very pleasing sounds, very delightful music, vocal and instrumental; but it never heard such music as will be heard in heaven. The heart of man can conceive of more than it has either seen or heard; but it never conceived of such things as will be enjoyed in the world above.

The door of access to heavenly glory is strait. The way is narrow. We must come in by the Door, Christ Jesus. The only way to God, the only way to heaven, the only way to glory is faith in the Lord Jesus Christ. Christ is the Only Way, the Righteous Way, and the Sure Way. Let none be satisfied with merely studying about the glory awaiting God's saints in heaven. Let us make certain we are in the Way that brings sinners there. Let us make our calling and election sure. Make certain you are in Christ.

Images Of Heavenly Glory

My soul, this curious house of clay,
Thy present frail abode;
Must quickly fall to worms a prey,
And thou return to God.

Canst thou, by faith, survey with joy
The change before it come?
And say, "Let death this house destroy,
I have a heavenly home!"

The Saviour, whom I then shall see
With new admiring eyes,
Already has prepared for me,
A mansion in the skies.

I feel this mud-walled cottage shake,
And long to see it fall;
That I my willing flight might take
To Him who is my All.

Burdened and groaning, then no more,
My rescued soul shall sing,
As up the shining path I soar,
"Death, death thou hast lost thy sting."

Dear Saviour, help us now to seek,
And know thy grace's power;
That we may all this language speak,
Before the dying hour.

John Newton

Going Home

As for me, I will behold thy face in righteousness: I shall be satisfied, when I awake, with thy likeness.

Psalm 17:15

Chapter 5

Heaven: The Place Of Satisfaction

Heaven is a place of satisfaction; complete, perfect, eternal satisfaction. All the purpose of Almighty God shall be fully satisfied in heaven. When all things are finished, when everything that must be has been, when the present heavens and earth have passed away and God has made all things new, when the wicked have been cast into hell forever and the saints of God have all been transformed into the image of his dear Son, when all things have been completely subdued to Christ, 'Then cometh the end'. Then Christ shall deliver up the whole company of the redeemed to God our Father, and God shall be 'all in all' (1 Corinthians 15:24-28). All God's elect shall be saved forever. God's glory shall be revealed in all things to all creatures. And our Lord Jesus Christ, who alone is worthy, shall have all pre-eminence for all eternity.

Christ Satisfied

In heaven the Lord Jesus Christ, God's dear Son, shall see of the travail of his soul and shall be satisfied (Isaiah 53:10, 11). The Lord Jesus Christ was made sin for us, that we might be made the righteousness of God in him. When he was made sin, he suffered all the horrible, ignominious wrath of Almighty God as the sinner's Substitute, so that God might be just and the Justifier of all who believe.

The agony and death of Christ is called by the prophet Isaiah, 'the travail of his soul'. Our Saviour's travail was unto death that he might give us eternal life. Isaiah assures us his death was not in vain. 'He shall see of the travail of his soul, and shall be satisfied'! Christ did not shed his blood for nothing. The cross of our Lord Jesus Christ shall never be discovered a miscarriage. In heaven's final glory all the intentions, purposes and designs of Christ in his death shall be satisfied. Every desire of his holy heart, which compelled him to lay down his life for us shall be fully satisfied. Every soul he loved with an everlasting love shall be with him in his glory. Every sinner for whom he suffered, bled and died under the wrath of God shall be thoroughly purged of all sin. Every person he undertook to save shall stand before him in perfect righteousness. The whole company of God's elect, for whom he became a Surety in the covenant of grace, shall be presented by him to his Father, 'holy, unblameable, and unreproveable' in his sight.

Believers Satisfied

And there, in our happy, eternal home, in our Father's house in heaven, every desire of the believer's heart shall be fully satisfied (Psalm 17:15). Nothing is a surer sign of God's wrath and of a man's reprobation than for God to give him satisfaction in this world and with this world. I pity the 'men of the world, which have their portion in this life', whom God has filled and satisfied with the treasures of the earth (Psalm 17:14), in whose heart 'he hath set the world' so that they cannot find him (Ecclesiastes 3:11).

For the renewed soul there is no possibility of satisfaction in this world. We need to be content with God's daily providence, knowing our Father is wise and good and what he does is best. But we find no satisfaction here. That which our hearts crave cannot be satisfied until we get to heaven. But there, in heaven with Christ, we shall be satisfied.

This is what David said. 'As for me, I will behold thy face in righteousness; I shall be satisfied, when I awake, with thy likeness.' I take David's words to imply there are two stages of satisfaction for God's saints in heaven. First, the satisfaction that is found in heaven between death and the resurrection when we shall behold our Saviour's face in righteousness, and second, the satisfaction that shall be found in heaven after the resurrection of the body when we shall awake in the likeness of our Redeemer.

Believers, as soon as they leave this world, find satisfaction for their souls in heaven. I keep stressing this because it needs to be stressed. In our day many who appear to be otherwise orthodox in their doctrine, have begun to teach the Adventists' doctrine of soul sleep. I will not now discuss all the ramifications of that evil doctrine. But it is a doctrine that robs God's people of comfort in the hour of their own death and with regard to their departed loved ones. Also, it is a doctrine that inspires undue attachment to this world. But more importantly, it is a doctrine directly contrary to the Word of God.

As we have seen repeatedly, the souls of believers, as soon as they are separated from their bodies, are immediately with Christ in heaven (2 Corinthians 5:8; Philippians 1:23), in a state of blessed happiness and satisfaction. It is this intermediate state of satisfaction, between death and the resurrection, that David referred to when he said, 'As for me, I will behold thy face in righteousness.'

> Soon as I draw my final breath,
> And close my mortal eyes in death,
> I shall with Christ in glory be,
> In righteousness, forever free!

As soon as we enter heaven we will find complete satisfaction for our souls in these six things.

1. God's Presence

When we enter heaven, we shall enter into the immediate presence of our God (Psalm 16:11).

Nothing in this world is more desirable and satisfying to believers than the knowledge and assurance of God's presence. We choose, with Moses, not to go anywhere without his presence (Exodus 33:15). It is our Lord's presence with us that makes the ordinance of public worship pleasing (Matthew 18:20). The presence of God comforts us in our trials (Isaiah 43:1-5). And our Lord's presence inspires all our service to him (Matthew 28:20). The presence of Christ with his church on earth makes one day in his temple more desirable than a thousand days spent anywhere else. His presence makes his tabernacles on earth amiable tabernacles (Psalm 84:1, 2, 10). We find satisfaction even here in this world, indeed, our highest satisfaction here upon earth, in the manifestation of God's presence with us.

How gloriously happy and satisfied those saints must be who have entered into the immediate presence of God in heaven, never to be separated from him again. Blessed indeed are those in heaven who have entered into perpetual, uninterrupted communion with the Triune God. The presence of God in heaven means that God's saints there enjoy perpetual satisfaction. What great and glorious fellowship they enjoy as they enter into the full experience of 'the grace of our Lord Jesus Christ, and the love of God, and the communion of the Holy Ghost'!

There is nothing in all the world so delightful to the hearts of believing sinners as sitting with Christ at his table, to be brought into his banqueting house, to smell the sweet spikenard of his grace, and have him display the banner of his love over them (Song of Solomon 2:4-6). There is nothing so glorious and satisfying in all the world as real worship! But imagine what it will be like in that world of glory to be in communion with God our Saviour forever! What satisfaction! What delight! What glory!

2. Conformed To Christ
In that glory world we call heaven, all who now long to be like Christ shall be satisfied, for we shall be perfectly conformed to our Redeemer.

Today we see him by faith. And beholding him by faith we 'are changed into the same image from glory to glory' by the Spirit of the Lord (2 Corinthians 3:18). But in heaven we shall see Christ clearly as he is. We shall have a full and perfect view of him, and when we see him as he is we shall be like him (1 John 3:2).

It was the great object of God in predestination, that we should be conformed to the image of his Son (Romans 8:29). In heaven, that which God predestinated before the worlds were made shall be brought to pass. We shall be like Christ perfectly. Every power and faculty of our souls shall be a perfect reflection of our all-glorious Saviour. Every faculty of the glorified soul shall be swallowed up in Christ. In our understanding, we shall have a clear and unclouded view of him. The thoughts of our minds will be always toward him. Our wills will be entirely submissive to, and conformed to, his will. The affection of our hearts will be set upon Christ and things above. Our memories will be fully stored with heavenly, spiritual things. We will have memories not of sorrow and pain, but of mercy and grace. John Gill wrote, 'There will be nothing irregular and disagreeable in the soul, in its motions, thoughts, and actions.'

3. Heavenly Conversation
Our souls will find satisfaction in heavenly conversation.

Heaven will be a place of much talk and conversation. There we shall carry on conversation both with the angels of God and with 'the spirits of just men made perfect'. How we will communicate in that state, I do not know. What the language of heaven is, I cannot tell. But we will communicate with one another freely, spiritually, and profitably about the things of God.

4. Perfect Knowledge
Our souls will be satisfied with perfect and complete knowledge in heaven.

'For now we see through a glass darkly; but then face to face: now I know in part; but then shall I know even as also I am known' (1 Corinthians 13:12). As soon as we drop this robe of flesh, everything that hinders us in spiritual knowledge shall be gone. Then we shall have perfect knowledge of God the Father in all his attributes and works, of the Son of God in all his offices, works and grace, of the Spirit of God in all his being and gracious operations, of the angels of God in all their secret missions of mercy for us, of the providence of God in all its intricate details, and of one another. I do not doubt we shall learn forever. Yet, even while learning, our knowledge will be crystal clear and pure. It will not be contaminated by sin and unbelief!

5. Perfect Holiness

We shall be satisfied with perfect holiness.

'As for me, I will behold thy face in righteousness.' In that blessed state our souls shall be entirely free from sin. The guilt of sin is now removed from us by the blood of Christ. But when we stand before God's throne we will be completely free from the pollution of sin, the dread of sinning again, the body of sin, the being of sin, and all the consequences of sin. In heaven, hard as it is to conceive now, there will not even be any more sorrow for sin, 'for God shall wipe away all tears' from our eyes!

That happy day cannot come soon enough, when we shall no longer groan and struggle with sin. In heaven, as soon as we leave this world, we shall be perfectly holy, completely unblameable, and unreproveable, without spot or blemish. We shall have no sinful thoughts, no impure desires, no evil inclinations, no wicked will. This holiness and freedom from sin will not in any measure be the result of our own free will or good works. We have none. It will be the result of God's work and his grace alone.

6. Perfect Peace

And in heaven, we shall be satisfied with perfect, eternal peace (Psalm 37:37).

Peace! Sweet peace! Nothing is more desirable and satisfying than peace. Perfect peace is given to all who trust Christ now. But what shall that peace be which we shall have when we enter into the joy of the Lord? (See Isaiah 57:1, 2; Matthew 25:21).

Immediately after death, God's saints enter into heaven to forever behold his face in righteousness and find perfect satisfaction in the presence of God, in conformity to Christ, in heavenly conversation, in perfect knowledge, in perfect holiness, and in perfect peace. Yet, there is another, even higher stage of heavenly glory.

Celestial Satisfaction

In the resurrection our bodies as well as our souls shall find perfect satisfaction in heavenly glory. David referred to the resurrection of the body when he said, 'I shall be satisfied, when I awake with thy likeness.' We often speak of the salvation of the soul. But the Bible never does. The Bible speaks of the salvation of people, the salvation of both the body and the soul. The salvation of God's elect will not be complete until Christ has redeemed our bodies from the grave at the resurrection (Romans 8:23; 1 Corinthians 1:30; Ephesians 1:14; 4:30; 1 Corinthians 15:41-58).

At the resurrection there will be a glory put upon the bodies of God's saints, as well as that which is put upon their souls. The purpose of God will not be satisfied, the soul travail of Christ will not be satisfied, and the hearts' desire of God's saints will not be satisfied until all the bodies of God's elect are saved and gathered into glory.

This body must be sown in the earth in corruption. It is a vile body, corrupted by sin. It shall be brought into the corruption of death and laid in corruption in the dust of the earth, where it must rot and decay. But this very same body must be raised up to glory in incorruption, where it will no more be corrupted by sin, disease, or death. 'This corruptible must put on incorruption, and this mortal must put on immortality'. Then shall death be swallowed up in victory!

This body must be sown in the earth in dishonour. If there is anything noble, appealing, and pleasing about it, it will quickly fade away. Soon this body will become fit only for the company of worms beneath the cold, dark sod of the earth. But it shall be raised in glory.

Yes, this body shall come forth from the grave in the perfection of beauty and comeliness, fashioned like unto the glorious body of Christ. And it shall shine like the sun in heaven.

This body of flesh must be sown in the earth in weakness. Soon it will lose all strength and vigour. In the end it shall be carried by pall-bearers to the grave. But it shall be raised in power. It shall be raised in strength and fitness, able to live forever without aging or getting weak, able to move quickly from place to place, even from earth to heaven in an instant, able to attend the service of God and the Lamb forever, without weakness and weariness. In the resurrection, we will never again have to complain that 'the spirit is willing, but the flesh is weak' (Matthew 26:41).

This body must be sown in the earth a natural body. By reason of sin, it is an animal-like body, supported by animal food. It must die as animals do (Ecclesiastes 3:19, 20). However, it shall be raised a spiritual body, subsisting like the angels of God forever, never to die again. Then our bodies will no longer be encumbrances to our souls as they are now. Then our bodies will assist us in spiritual services. They will be fitted for spiritual employments and suited to spiritual worship. In our resurrection bodies we shall be satisfied.

When our bodies are raised from the earth and united with our souls, in the perfection of our whole being we shall be brought into a heavenly state of everlasting glory. I know I cannot adequately describe the glorious satisfaction that awaits us. But it is so blessed, I must try to give some sense of it.

Clear Vision

In heaven's glory we shall see the living God (Job 19:25-27). Now we walk by faith, then we shall walk by sight. Now we see God by faith, in, through and by his Word, then we shall behold his face in righteousness. We shall see him face to face, as he is (2 Corinthians 5:7; Psalm 17:15; 1 Corinthians 13:12; 1 John 3:2).

I do not mean that we shall see God physically, in the essence of his Being, and comprehend him. That is not possible because God is the infinite, incomprehensible Spirit. But I do mean we shall have a clear, unclouded apprehension of God's perfections and glory as we behold the full revelation of God in Christ, the God-man. We will see all the fulness of the Godhead bodily in Christ (Colossians 2:9). As we behold Christ, we will perfectly apprehend God the Father in all he is and all he has done, God the Son in all he is and all he has done, and God the Holy Spirit in all he is and all he has done. 'In my flesh shall I see God'! 'Then shall I be satisfied'!

In heaven's glory we will see all the holy angels. We will see the angels in their shining forms, ranks, and orders; those thrones, dominions, principalities, and powers made by Christ to be ministering spirits sent forth to minister to those whom he chose to be heirs of salvation. We will see those sons of God, those morning-stars who sang together and shouted for joy when God laid the foundations of the earth. We shall see those bright spirits who sang at Christ's incarnation, attended him in his ascension, and will return with him when he comes to judge the world in righteousness.

All God's saints will see and know one another in this glorious world of bliss. Just before he died someone asked Martin Luther, 'Sir, will we know one another in the other world?' Luther answered, 'As Adam knew Eve to be bone of his bone and flesh of his flesh by the revelation of God, though he had never seen her before, so shall the saints of God know one another in heaven.' As the apostles knew Moses and Elijah on the mount with Christ, though they had never seen them, or even a picture or description of them before, so shall we know the saints of God in heaven. In heaven we shall know parents, wives, husbands, children, and friends far more perfectly than ever we knew them on the earth.

There will be no strangers in heaven. If there were a stranger in the heavenly company, freedom and joy would be greatly hindered. Who is free around a stranger? In heaven's glory when the bodies of God's saints are raised up to glory we shall see and know one another and all God's saints. We shall all see the Bride, the Lamb's wife, in all the beauty which God has given her. We shall see and know every believer. And we shall love and esteem them all perfectly.

Glorious Liberty

Here is another aspect of heavenly satisfaction. In heaven's glory we shall possess everything that is good, and be free from everything that is evil (Revelation 22:4, 5). Total deliverance from sin, freedom from Satan's temptations, deliverance from troublesome, oppressive, wicked men, freedom from all afflictions, total freedom from distress and all that causes distress, will be ours forever. Surely, this is what Paul had in mind when he wrote of us being 'delivered from the bondage of corruption into the glorious liberty of the sons of God' (Romans 8:21). There will be no more fightings without, or fears within, no more doubts, misgivings, no more unbelief! Everlasting joy shall be our portion. Sorrow and sighing shall flee away!

Heavenly Enjoyments

Once more, the saints of God will find satisfaction in their resurrection glory in their everlasting employments. Then all our conversations will be holy conversations. We shall live in the perpetual worship and praise of our God. And we shall enjoy the everlasting perfection of love. This heavenly glory is the gift of God's pure, free grace in Christ. Now, if we look for such great and glorious things in the world to come, it ought to affect the way we live upon the earth today (2 Peter 3:11; Colossians 3:1-4). Such a hope of glory ought to inspire in us the utmost consecration to our Lord Jesus Christ.

1. Ye souls that trust in Christ, rejoice;
Your sins are all forgiven;
Let every Christian lift his voice,
And sing the joys of heaven.

2. Heaven is that holy, happy, place,
Where sin no more defiles;
Where God unveils his blissful face,
And looks, and loves, and smiles.

3. [Where Jesus, Son of man and God,
Triumphant from his wars,
Walks in rich garments dipped in blood,
And shows his glorious scars;]

4. [Where ransomed sinners sound God's praise
The angelic host among;
Sing the rich wonders of his grace,
And Jesus leads the song;]

5. [Where saints are freed from every load
Of passions or of pains;
God dwells in them, and they in God;
And love for ever reigns.]

Heaven: The Place Of Satisfaction

6. Lord, as thou show'st thy glory there,
Make known thy grace to us;
And heaven will not be wanting here
While we can hymn thee thus:

7. Jesus, our dear Redeemer, died
That we might be forgiven;
Rose that we might be justified,
And sends the Spirit from heaven.

Joseph Hart

Going Home

Here is the patience of the saints: here are they that keep the commandments of God, and the faith of Jesus. And I heard a voice from heaven saying unto me, Write, Blessed are the dead which die in the Lord from henceforth: Yea, saith the Spirit, that they may rest from their labours; and their works do follow them.

Revelation 14:12, 13

Chapter 6

'Blessed Are The Dead, Which Die In The Lord'

How often we have stood by the bed of a dying friend or relative. Our hearts ache to lose any who are dear to us. We hurt for the husband or wife, parents, children, and others who will miss the love, companionship, and aide of the faithful one who is passing out of this world. Yet, as we watch our friends leave this world of sin and sorrow, knowing they are entering into heaven's everlasting glory, knowing they are falling asleep in the arms of their Saviour, we say, 'Blessed are the dead, which die in the Lord'.

When John heard those words from heaven, he did not have such a picture before him. Far from it. John had in his mind pictures of men and women dying in tormenting circumstances as martyrs. He had before him the picture of those dying because they worshipped Christ and received not the mark of the beast, neither in their foreheads nor in their right hands; men and women who were put to death because they would not deny Christ and his gospel. He says, with regard to those who were thrown to lions, those who died upon the rack in a loathsome dungeon, or were cast tied and bound into fast flowing rivers; those who were burned at the stake, and all those countless martyrs who have been tortured to death for their faith in Christ, 'Blessed are the dead which die in the Lord.'

C. H. Spurgeon stated the matter beautifully. 'Wheresoever on this earth, whether among the snows of Piedmont's valleys or in the fair fields of France, saints have died by sword or famine, or fire or massacre, for the testimony of Jesus, because they would not bear the mark of the beast ... this voice is heard sounding out of the third heaven, 'Blessed are the dead which die in the Lord'. 'Precious in the sight of the Lord is the death of his saints' (Psalm 116:15).

Precious Deaths

Yes, the psalmist sang, 'Precious in the sight of the Lord is the death of his saints.' Those who die in the Lord have entered into a state of eternal blessedness. The death of a believer is precious to God and blessed to him. It does not matter when a believer dies, where he dies, by what means he dies, or under what conditions he dies. The blessedness of the believer's death is that he dies in the Lord.

I once heard Pastor Henry Mahan relating a conversation he had with an old man in his congregation before service one evening. The aging saint said to his pastor, 'I'd lots rather be going out of this world than coming in. We've got things backwards. We rejoice at the birth of a child and weep at the death of an old man. We ought to weep when a child is born into this world and rejoice at the death of the old man if he is in Christ.'

Very, very soon, we must leave this world. 'Is there not an appointed time to man upon earth? Are not his days also like the days of a hireling?' We would be wise to take our minds off the cares and troubles, as well as the joys and riches of this world and look across the brief sea of time to eternity, to that future world so surely, perhaps nearly, awaiting us. Looking at things from the believer's perspective, we say with John, 'Blessed are the dead which die in the Lord.'

Of Whom Is This Said?

Of whom are these words spoken? The voice which John heard from heaven declared, 'Blessed are the dead which die in the Lord from henceforth.' That is to say, Those who die in the Lord are blessed, from the moment of their death, eternally. I want to know who those people are who die in the Lord, who are blessed forever. I want to be one of them. Who are they? Verse 12 tells us. 'Here is the patience of the saints: here are they that keep the commandments of God, and the faith of Jesus.'

Those who are blessed of God in death are the saints of God on earth. Heaven is the land of saints. None but saints can enter therein. Since death does nothing to change a person's character, if we would be numbered among the saints in heaven we must be made saints on earth. Yet, by nature we are all sinners. How can sinners be made saints? Only a work of God's almighty grace can make a sinner a saint.

A saint is one who is holy. Nothing short of a work of God's own hand can transform an unholy man into a holy man. Nothing but grace can make a sinner a saint. That work of grace which makes hell-bent sinners to be the saints of God is twofold. First, we must be redeemed by the precious blood of Christ. Our sins have to be put away. We must be justified, made righteous, by divine imputation (Romans 3:21-24). Christ has done this for all who trust him (Titus 2:14; Hebrews 1:3; 9:26). Then, second, we must be regenerated, set apart, sanctified, born again, and given a new nature by the Spirit of God (Ephesians 2:1-9; Titus 3:4-7). If we would enter into heaven, we must be made partakers of Christ's holiness (Hebrews 12:14). Being sanctified by the grace of God, believers, that is saints, set themselves apart and consecrate themselves to the Lord by faith in him, devoting themselves to him as willing bond slaves (Exodus 21:1-6; 2 Corinthians 8:5).

Those who are blessed in death are those who live in the patience of faith, 'the patience of the saints'. Believers are men and women of patience. They endure the troubles of life, the temptations of Satan, and the trials of faith with the patience of faith.

The word 'patience' here means 'endurance'. Those who are crowned in heaven endure their crosses on earth. Many who would be saints, when they are faced with a cross, exchange sainthood for ease. God's saints do not give up. They endure. They patiently run their race in faithfulness (Hebrews 12:1). They patiently endure adversity in faithfulness (Luke 21:19). They patiently wait for Christ in faithfulness (Romans 8:25; Hebrews 10:36). The basis of this patience is the Word of God (Romans 15:4).

That man or woman is blessed in death who keeps the commandments of God in life. We know that John is not saying, 'Obedience to the law is a condition for salvation.' We read in God's book, 'By the deeds of the law shall no flesh be justified in his sight' (Romans 3:20). Salvation is by grace alone. Legal works have nothing to do with it (Romans 11:5, 6; Galatians 5:1-4). John is not suggesting that believers are to put themselves back under the yoke of the Mosaic law, 'because we are not under law but under grace' (Romans 6:15).

What John is telling us is that the believer, the child of God, the saint of God, is one whose life is governed by God's Word (1 John 5:1-4). The believer is one who lives by the rule of God's Word. He keeps the commandments of the gospel (1 John 3:23, 24), obeys God from a principle of love and gratitude, and keeps and observes the ordinances of Christ. To the believer nothing revealed, taught, or commanded by his Lord is non-essential. He counts every word from God precious.

Those men and women who are blessed in death are, 'They that keep the faith of Jesus.' God promises salvation, eternal life, and everlasting, heavenly blessedness to those who persevere in faith (Colossians 1:21-23; Hebrews 3:6, 14; 10:38). All true believers persevere in the doctrine of faith which is nothing less than the gospel of Jesus Christ, and in the grace of faith (Matthew 10:22). This faith is called, 'the faith of Jesus', because it is the faith which Christ gives and the faith of which he is the Object.

Those who are, upon their death, forever blessed of God are men and women who are 'in the Lord'. That is the great, essential, all-telling point. Those people could not have died in the Lord had they not lived in the Lord.

Settle this matter now. Are you in Christ? Is he all your salvation and all your desire? Are you hanging upon him as a coat hangs upon a nail? Are you in the Beloved? Are you in Christ by the vital union of faith, as branches are in the vine? Blessed indeed is that man, that women who is in Christ! If you are in Christ, you are accepted of God; for we are 'accepted in the Beloved'. If you are not in Christ, you cannot be accepted at all.

To be in Christ is to live upon him by faith, drawing life and grace from him. The Scriptures speak of us being grafted into Christ (Romans 9:24). Wherever a branch is grafted into a tree, two cuts must be made, one in the tree and one in the branch. So it is with those who are grafted into Christ. He was wounded to death as our Substitute, and every believer is cut in his heart in Holy Spirit conviction. The wounded sinner is bound to the wounded Saviour by the Holy Spirit and from him draws life. To be in Christ by faith is to

81

have evidence and proof that God has put you in Christ by divine grace (Hebrews 11:1).

Turn this thought over in your heart and mind. If you trust Christ, it is because God has put you in Christ. To be in Christ is to be in his heart as a bride is in the heart of her husband, in his hands as your Surety, in his loins as your Representative before God, in his fold as your Shepherd, and in his body as your Head. To be in Christ is to be saved forever and kept in absolute security.

> Once in Christ, in Christ forever!
> None from Him our souls can sever.
> While His power and grace endure,
> All who trust Him are secure.

Of whom are these words spoken? 'Blessed are the dead which die in the Lord.' They are spoken to God's saints, to those who live in patience, to those who keep the commandments of God, to those that keep the faith of Jesus, to those who are in the Lord.

What Blessedness?

What is the blessedness of believers in death? Obviously, I cannot begin to tell what eye has not seen, ear has not heard, and the heart of man has not imagined, which God has prepared for them that love him. The blessedness of heavenly glory is infinitely greater than our feeble minds can imagine. But John does reveal, by divine inspiration, something of the blessedness awaiting every believer at death. 'Blessed are the dead which die in the Lord from henceforth: Yea, saith the Spirit, that they may rest from their labours.'

The believer is blessed in his dying, no matter how, when, or where he dies. We have abundant evidence of this fact in Scripture.

'Blessed Are The Dead, Which Die In The Lord'

Both Job and Paul were blessed in the prospect of death (Job 19:25-27; 2 Timothy 1:12; 4:6-8). David and Stephen were blessed in the experience of it (2 Samuel 23:5; Acts 7:56-60). Indeed, every sinner saved by grace shall be blessed of God in the event of death. 'To be absent from the body is to be present with the Lord.'

God's saints are forever blessed after they die, 'From henceforth'. 'We have a building of God, an house not made with hands, eternal in the heavens' (2 Corinthians 5:1). 'God shall wipe away all tears from their eyes.' Once we have left this world, we shall have forever left behind us every remnant and evil consequence of sin. In the glory land, there shall be 'no more weeping, no more sorrow, and no more pain' because there shall be no more sin.

Once we have dropped this robe of flesh we shall rest from our labours. I do not to understand this to mean the saints of God in heaven have no more service to render to Christ. Not at all. Heaven is a place of unending service. But there we shall rest from the labour of service. In heaven's glory, there will be no ignorant ones to teach, no erring ones to rebuke, no despondency to comfort, no weaknesses to strengthen, no error to oppose, no needy souls to help, no enemies to engage, no fences to mend, no strife to heal, no sick to visit, no bereaved to console, no straying to correct, no sinners to convert, and no tears to dry. We shall rest from our labours.

The word translated 'labours' has the idea of woe attached to it. It could be read, 'they rest from the woe of their labours'. In this world, all we do for Christ has a certain measure of woe connected with it. When John says, we shall rest from our labours, he means we shall rest from all the toils, sorrows, faults, discouragements, and disappointments connected with our labour in this world. 'Blessed are the dead which die in the Lord from henceforth: Yea, saith the Spirit, that they may rest from their labours; and their works do follow them.'

Works Do Follow

What does the believer's works have to do with his eternal, heavenly blessedness? We know our inheritance in heaven is the free gift of God's grace to which we have been predestinated. We know it has been purchased for us with Christ's own blood, and claimed for us by Christ our Representative (Ephesians 1:11, 14). We who believe are 'heirs of God and joint-heirs with Christ'. All the glory and blessedness Christ possesses in heaven today as the God-man, as our Surety, shall be ours forever by grace (John 17:5, 22). Nothing in this heavenly blessedness is earned or merited by, or given to us upon, the basis of our works. It is all of grace. Yet, the text says, 'and their works do follow them.' What does it mean? What do our works for Christ on earth have to do with our blessedness with Christ in heaven?

Our works do not go before us, as a forerunner, to prepare a place for us in heaven. Christ is our Forerunner. He went to prepare a place for us. Our works merit nothing from God, except wrath and death, because our best works are but sin. Our works do not come beside us as a ground of confidence and acceptance with God. The wicked lean upon their works, boast of their works and plead with God for acceptance upon the basis of their works (Matthew 7:22, 23). The righteous are unaware of any good works performed by them (Matthew 25:34-40).

However the works of faithful men and women are not insignificant or unimportant, as many seem to think for, 'their works do follow them.' This simply means that the fruits of their works follow them in the earth and follow them into heaven. What a blessed promise this is! Those who are the beneficiaries of the believer's works follow them to heaven. Children follow their parents, who taught them the gospel, in the path of faith to heaven. Hearers follow their pastors, who have faithfully preached Christ to them, both in the church below and into the Church above. Multitudes who never met on earth will follow humble saints into heaven, who served Christ on earth, never thinking they did anything of any usefulness to anyone.

> Blest are the dead that die in Christ,
> For they are with Him now!
> The glories they now have in heaven,
> No mortal here can know.
>
> Soon as the ransomed soul is freed,
> From this poor, mortal frame,
> Before we know it's gone, it is
> With Christ, praising His name.
>
> Faith tries, but here cannot quite see,
> The things God has prepared
> For those He chose, redeemed, and called,
> Who now in heaven appear.
>
> We'll now rejoice this much to know,
> They are completely blest!
> Freed from all sorrow, pain, and sin,
> With Jesus Christ they rest!
>
> Our friends their Saviour fully see,
> And all His glory share.
> Let us be followers of the Lamb;
> And we will join them there.

'Blessed are the dead which die in the Lord'!

Going Home

And if children, then heirs; heirs of God, and joint-heirs with Christ; if so be that we suffer with him, that we may be also glorified together.

Romans 8:17

Chapter 7

'Heirs Of God'

Every text in Romans chapter 8 seems to be a phrase bursting with meaning. It seems to be an inexhaustible mine overflowing with glorious gospel truth. Every word seems to echo, 'Grace'! 'Grace'! 'Grace'! Everything directs our thoughts to the grace of God and shows forth the glory of God. Starting at verse one, Paul sets before us a golden ladder. Each step seems to ascend higher and higher. From justification, he rises to regeneration. From regeneration, he rises to sanctification. From sanctification, he rises to glorification. In glorification, he declares God's elect to be 'heirs of God and joint-heirs with Jesus Christ'! To all who believe on the Lord Jesus Christ there is the promise of an inheritance that is incorruptible, eternal, undefiled, and 'fadeth not away'. What can this mean? What is it to be an heir of God?

Without question, this inheritance is the only inheritance worth having. Every other inheritance is unsatisfying and disappointing.

The riches of this world, for which men labour so feverishly, are sure to bring with them many cares. They can never cure an aching heart, ease a troubled conscience, or relieve the burdens of a guilty soul. The riches of this world cannot prevent sickness, bereavement, separation, and death. They cannot even secure temporary happiness or domestic tranquillity; but there shall never be any disappointment among the heirs of God in heaven.

The inheritance spoken of here is the only inheritance that can be kept forever. All others, if they have not vanished before, must be left at the hour of death. Howard Hughes carried no more with him to the grave than Lazarus (Luke 16:19-31). That is not the case with the heirs of God. Our inheritance in Christ is eternal (Hebrews 9:15).

The inheritance awaiting God's saints in glory is the only inheritance there is which is within the reach of all who desire it. Most people in this world will never be able to obtain great wealth or attain prominence, no matter how hard they strive for them. Yet, glory, honour, and eternal life are set before sinners in the gospel and freely given to all who accept them on God's terms. 'Whosoever will' may be an 'heir of God and joint-heir with Jesus Christ'! Yes, all who trust Christ are the children of God; and all who are the children of God are 'heirs of God and joint heirs with Jesus Christ.'

If Children, Heirs

All who are the children of God are the heirs of God. 'If children, then heirs.' If we are the children of God, then we are the heirs of God. If we are not God's children, then we are not God's heirs. Shocking as it is for many to be informed of it, the fact is, not all people are the children of God. We are all God's creatures; but we are not all God's children. This heirship does not come as the result of natural creation or family descent. The Holy Spirit does not say, 'if creatures, then heirs', or 'if children of Abraham, then heirs'.

'Heirs Of God'

Grace does not run in bloodlines. Grace is the free gift of God (John 1:12, 13; Romans 9:7-13). Neither human merit nor religious rituals are the basis of heirship (Galatians 4:30; Romans 4:9-12). It is not written, 'if servants, then heirs', or 'if circumcised or baptized, then heirs'.

The Holy Spirit tells us plainly that the one condition of heirship with Christ is this 'if children, then heirs'. Perhaps you ask yourself, 'How can I know whether or not I am a child of God? How can I know whether or not I am born again, born from above?' God provides us with very clear answers to those questions in his Word. There is no guess work to this important thing.

Five Characteristics
Here are five characteristics of all who are children of God. If these things are true of us, we are the children of God, born again by almighty grace, and heirs of God. If these things are not true of us, then we are yet 'children of wrath even as others'.

1. Believers
All who are born of God are believers in the Lord Jesus Christ. All who are the children of God, all who are saved by the grace of God, all who are 'heirs of God and joint-heirs with Christ', believe on the Lord Jesus Christ (John 1:12).

If you trust the Lord Jesus Christ alone as your Lord and Saviour, if you look to Christ alone for acceptance with God, your faith in him is the fruit and evidence of his work of grace in you (Hebrews 11:1). Our faith in Christ is the fruit and evidence of the fact we have been born of the Holy Spirit and we are the children of God (Galatians 4:6, 7).

2. Spiritually Led

All who are the children of God are led by the Spirit of God (Romans 8:14).

The Holy Spirit leads those who are Christ's. There is a movement in their hearts, lives, and affections which they feel, though they may not be able to explain it. It is a movement which is always in the same direction. The Holy Spirit always leads us away from ourselves to Christ: away from our sin to his blood; away from our righteousness to his righteousness; away from self-confidence to the confidence of faith in Christ; away from our feelings to his Word; away from our works to his work. The Spirit of God also leads believers by providence, through the counsel of the Word, and by the power of his grace. He guides them in the ways of God, in paths of righteousness, and to the throne of grace.

3. Perfect Liberty

All who are born again by the quickening power and grace of God the Holy Spirit have the blessed liberty of the sons of God (Romans 8:1-4, 15).

We have been delivered from the slavish fear of God's holy judgment which is caused by the guilt of sin and the terror of the law. We have been redeemed from the guilt that caused Adam to hide 'himself in the trees of the garden' and made Cain 'go out from the presence of the Lord'. Though we fear God in the sense of holding him in the highest reverence, believers are no longer afraid of God in the sense of being terrified of him, or his judgment. Sinners though we are, we are not afraid of God's holiness, justice, and majesty.

We see God now in the full glory of his holy Being and have peace, because we see him reconciled through the blood of his own dear Son. We see all his glorious attributes displayed and honoured in the death of Christ as our Substitute. We now draw near to God in prayer and speak to him with the confidence and peace of a child to his father. We now serve the Lord our God, not from a sense of fear, but from a sense of love and gratitude. We have exchanged the spirit of bondage for the Spirit of liberty. We have given up the spirit of fear for the Spirit of love. We have put off the spirit of obligation and put on the Spirit of gratitude. We have dropped the spirit of law and taken up the Spirit of grace.

4. Witness Of The Spirit

All who are born of God, all who are the children of God have the witness of the Spirit that they are the children of God (Romans 8:16; 1 Corinthians 1:22; 2 Corinthians 5:5; Ephesians 1:13; 4:30; 1 John 5:10).

The Holy Spirit has sprinkled our hearts with the blood of Christ. The blood applied by the Spirit assures us of Christ's sufficiency for all our needs. He gives us witness by the Word, assuring us our sins have been put away, peace with God is restored, heaven's door is opened before us, and hell's pit is forever shut against us. We have, by the witness of the Spirit, what the world can never have, 'a good hope through grace' (2 Thessalonians 2:16).

5. Endure Sufferings With Christ

The sons of God voluntarily take part in the sufferings of Christ.

It is written, 'If so be that we suffer with him, that we may be also glorified together' (Romans 8:17). We seek to know our Saviour 'in the fellowship of his sufferings' (Philippians 3:10). And all God's children voluntarily take up their cross and follow their Master. They 'follow the Lamb withersoever he goeth', regardless of cost or consequence.

Same Reason, Extent, And Fulness

All who are the children of God are the heirs of God; and all who are the children of God are the heirs of God for the same reason, to the same extent, and to the same fulness. Many believe that while all God's children are his heirs, some will inherit a scanty portion as naughty sons and daughters while others will have a large, honourable, and happy portion as obedient children. Nothing could be further from the truth. Our inheritance in heaven is not conditioned upon our works, be they good or bad, but upon our relationship to God. 'If children, then heirs'! The issue is determined by the word 'if'. If we are the Lord's children, then no doubt can exist regarding our heavenly inheritance.

There is no such thing as degrees of reward in heaven. There are no slums in the heavenly Jerusalem. There are no uncrowned princes in heaven. Whoever he was who invented the doctrine of degrees of reward in heaven knew nothing about the doctrine of grace in the gospel. The whole system smacks of the popish doctrines of indulgences and purgatory. It is but another subtle system of works religion.

Not all of God's children are prophets, apostles, preachers, teachers, evangelists, or even well-instructed. Not all are rich and influential in spiritual gifts and works. They are not all strong and useful; but they are all heirs of God, and equally so.

All are children of the same Father, loved with the same love, to the same degree. There are no degrees to our Father's love. All are blessed with the same blessings from eternity. Our Father will not take away what he has already given us; and he has already given us all things in Christ before the world was made (Ephesians 1:3). All are accepted upon the same grounds, for the same reason, to the same degree (Ephesians 1:6). All are equally related to the Elder Brother, the Firstborn Son, the Lord Jesus Christ, through whom the inheritance comes. All have already obtained the inheritance in Christ representatively (Ephesians 1:11; Hebrews 6:20).

There is no room for works in the system of grace (Romans 11:6). Our glorification will no more be determined by our works than our election, redemption, justification, regeneration, and sanctification are determined by our works. Salvation is all of grace. If heavenly glory is the ultimate end of salvation, and it is, then our works have nothing to do with it.

'Heirs Of God'

The Holy Spirit describes all believers as 'heirs of God'. Think of the implications of that fact. Our inheritance is divinely great. This is what the Scriptures declare consistently. 'He that overcometh shall inherit all things' (Revelation 21:7). 'All things are yours' (2 Corinthians 3:21).

If we are the children of God, then we are heirs of God's salvation (Hebrews 1:14), heirs of eternal life (Titus 3:7), heirs of promise (Hebrews 6:17), heirs of the grace of life (1 Peter 3:7), heirs of righteousness (Hebrews 11:7), and heirs of the kingdom (James 2:5). There are no partial heirs.

If we are heirs of God, our inheritance is an inheritance of infinite proportion, too. To be heirs of God is to be heirs of all God possesses, heirs of all he is, heirs of God himself, and heirs of all to which the Lord Jesus Christ, as the God-man, our Mediator is heir. He has given to all his elect all the glory God the Father gave to him as the result of his perfect obedience to God as our Representative (John 17:5, 22).

Joint-Heirs With Christ

Between Christ and his people there subsists such a gloriously mysterious union that all believers are joint-heirs with Christ himself.

'If children, then heirs; heirs of God, and joint-heirs with Jesus Christ.' This is grace indeed. God has pardoned us, received us into his house, adopted us as his sons, made us all his heirs, and has made us to be joint-heirs with his own dear Son. As justification is union and communion with Christ in his righteousness, and sanctification is union and communion with Christ in his holiness, so glorification will be union and communion with Christ in his Sonship.

Our inheritance with Christ is an inheritance worthy of the Son of God. What an inheritance that must be! It is such an inheritance as the Father reserves for and gives to his well-beloved Son in whom he is well-pleased. Our worthiness to obtain this glorious inheritance is our union with the Lord Jesus Christ. Our only worthiness to approach God in any way, at any time, is Christ.

Yes, in Christ every believer is worthy to obtain this inheritance (Colossians 1:12). We have been made worthy by the work of God's free grace in Christ, who brought in perfect righteousness for us by his holy life and fully paid our debt by his sin-atoning death. Our everlasting inheritance in glory with Christ is a matter of absolute certainty. Our union with him secures it. His title deed to glory is ours. The two are indivisible. His prayer for us claimed it for us. He has gone into heaven to prepare it for us, and holds it in our name, as our Forerunner. He is coming again to bring us into the blessed possession of it.

I really do not know what to expect when we have obtained our inheritance (1 John 3:2); but some things are both certain and clearly revealed in the Word of God. When we have been raised from the dead and transformed into Christ's likeness, when we enter into his glory there will be nothing in eternity to sadden our hearts or dampen our spirits (Revelation 21:3, 4). 'Then we shall know, even as we are known.' We shall say an eternal good-bye to sin, Satan, and sorrow, and attain perfect holiness. We shall enter into perfect rest (Hebrews

4:9). Yet, we shall serve the Lord perfectly (Revelation 7:15). We shall live in perfect communion with one another. We shall be totally satisfied when we shall see our Saviour face to face (Psalm 17:15).

Going Home

And God shall wipe away all tears from their eyes; and there shall be no more death, neither sorrow, nor crying, neither shall there be any more pain: for the former things are passed away.

Revelation 21:4

Chapter 8

Will There Be Degrees Of Reward In Heaven?

Will there be degrees of reward in heaven? That is a question about which there has been much controversy throughout the history of the church. Many men, whose doctrine has been thoroughly biblical in other areas, have been in serious error concerning rewards. I know I will not settle the controversy surrounding this question in this study. However, it is my responsibility to teach those things which become sound doctrine and build up the saints of God in the faith of Christ, so those taught by me will not be 'tossed to and fro, and carried about with every wind of doctrine, by the sleight of men, and cunning craftiness.' My purpose in this study therefore is threefold. I want to glorify and honour our great God, establish you who read these lines in the faith of Christ, and show sinners the way of salvation by grace alone.

Salvation involves and entails all that is required to bring a sinner from the ruins of the fall into the glory of heaven. This salvation, in its entirety, is the work of God's free grace. That is the foundation upon which we build all our doctrine. Salvation is by grace alone, through faith alone, in Christ alone. No part of salvation can be, in any measure attributed to the will, worth or works of man (2 Timothy 1:9; Ephesians 2:8, 9; Romans 11:6). If it is possible to separate heavenly rewards from salvation then you might talk about degrees of reward; but if heaven and the glorious inheritance of the saints in heaven is only the consummation of salvation then to talk of degrees of reward in heaven is to teach salvation by works.

The Doctrine

What is the doctrine of those who teach degrees of reward in heaven? I realize some men who teach this doctrine may have some slightly different opinions than others; but basically this is their doctrine. Lest I be accused of putting words in their mouths, let me quote directly from one of the leading proponents of this doctrine. The following are the words of Merrill F. Unger.

> Rewards are offered by God to a believer on the basis of faithful service rendered after salvation. It is clear from Scripture that God offers to the lost salvation and for the faithful service of the saved rewards. Often in theological thinking salvation and rewards are confused. However, these two terms must be carefully distinguished. Salvation is a free gift (John 4:10; Romans 6:23; Ephesians 2:8, 9), while rewards are earned by works (Matthew 10:42; Luke 19:17; 1 Corinthians 9:24, 25; 2 Timothy 4:7, 8). Rewards will be dispensed at the Judgment Seat of Christ (2 Corinthians 5:10; Romans 14:10). The doctrine of rewards is inseparably connected with God's grace. A soul being saved on the basis of divine grace, there is no room for the building up of merit on the part of the believer. Yet, God

recognizes an obligation on his part to reward his saved ones for their service to him. Nothing can be done to merit salvation, but what the believer has achieved for God's glory God recognizes in his great faithfulness with rewards at the Judgment Seat of Christ.

Mr. Unger gives a fair representation of what those men teach who teach degrees of reward in heaven. They teach …

1. Salvation is limited to the initial experience of conversion. However, that is not the doctrine of the New Testament (2 Corinthians 2:10; 2 Timothy 1:9; Romans 13:11; 1 Peter 2:4; Matthew 10:22). We cannot separate one part of salvation from another. It is one package. It is all connected. Those who have election have redemption. Those who have justification have sanctification. Those who have been given grace shall be given glory, (Romans 8:28-30). All spiritual blessings belong to all God's elect (Ephesians 1:3, 4).

2. It is possible for a person to be saved and not be a faithful servant of the Lord Jesus Christ. Popular as the doctrine is among religionists, it is directly contrary to the Word of God. All believers are voluntary subjects and servants to Christ their Lord and King (Luke 14:25-33).

3. Men, by their service to God, put God under obligation to reward them! That is utter nonsense. Is it possible for a sinful man or woman to do anything to merit God's favour and earn God's blessing? Can a mere man oblige the Almighty?

4. There will be two judgment days, one for believers and another for unbelievers. Those people must make the Bible fit their doctrine so they teach that there are two second comings of Christ,

one secret and one open and public, two second resurrections, one secret and one open and public, and two judgments, one for believers, 'The Judgment Seat of Christ' and one for unbelievers, 'The Great White Throne'.

5. Believers will yet have to suffer for their sins! This is one of the most horrendous aspects of the doctrine of degrees of reward in heaven. It puts some of God's saints through an everlasting state of purgatory in heaven, declaring that some must forever suffer punishment and loss for their sins after conversion! The Word of God, however, emphatically declares that God will never charge his people with sin (Romans 4:8; 8:32-34).

Inevitable Implications
The teaching that there will be degrees of reward in heaven has some undeniable and inevitable consequences. If the doctrine of degrees of reward in heaven is accepted and believed, then it must be equally acknowledged that:

1. Heaven's glory is not the reward of grace, but the payment of a debt.
2. Heaven is not a place of unmingled joy, but of mingled joy and grief.
3. God does withhold some good things from them that walk uprightly, and some evil shall fall upon the just (Psalm 84:11; Proverbs 12:21).
4. The blood of Christ and the righteousness of Christ is not alone sufficient for our acceptance with God.
5. Some part of God's favour, some of the blessings of God must be earned by us!

Will There Be Degrees Of Reward In Heaven?

A Doctrine Opposed

Why must we be so dogmatically opposed to this doctrine? We oppose it because it is without foundation in the Word of God. Not one passage referred to in support of this doctrine even hints of some saints having more glory and some having less glory in heaven. Not one of the crowns mentioned in the Bible are said to be given only to certain believers. They are all given to all believers, see Revelation 4:10.

The doctrine of degrees of reward in heaven is totally contrary to the plainest statements of Holy Scripture (Matthew 20:1-16, see especially verse 12; John 17:5, 22; Romans 8:17, 29; Ephesians 1:3; 5:25-27; Jude 24; 1 John 3:2). Can there be degrees of holiness, degrees of perfection, degrees of faultlessness, degrees of glorification? Of course not!

The doctrine of degrees of reward in heaven makes service to Christ a legal, mercenary thing. It promotes pride and threatens punishment. It is a merit-based, reward-inspired, legal service. God's people are not hired, but willing servants. The soldiers in Christ's army are not mercenaries, but volunteers.

The doctrine of rewards robs the Lord Jesus Christ of the glory of his grace and makes room for human flesh to boast before God. If we have done something that puts Almighty God under obligation to reward us, then we have a right to boast in his presence. If we do something by which we merit a higher standing than others in glory, we have every right to boast of our achievements. Yet, anyone who reads the Word of God knows better. Indeed, anyone who has experienced the grace of God shudders at the thought of boasting in his presence (1 Corinthians 4:7).

The doctrine of degrees of reward in glory has the obnoxious odour of works about it; and there is no room for works in the kingdom of grace and in the presence of God. It is not possible to worship God on an altar of hewn stone (Exodus 20:25). There is no room for the baggage of works at the strait gate and on the narrow way.

One Text

There is one text of Holy Scripture which both destroys the doctrine of degrees of reward and assures every believer of an everlasting fulness of joy in glory. Read Revelation 21:4, 'And God shall wipe away all tears from their eyes; and there shall be no more death, neither sorrow, nor crying, neither shall there be any more pain: for the former things are passed away.'

This text implies there is much weeping in the way to heaven, and there is. Faith in Christ brings deliverance from all curse and condemnation, but not from pain and sorrow. There are many things believers suffer in this world along with other men, such as pain and sickness, both physical and mental, domestic troubles, financial losses, bereavements, and much more. Because this world is a world of sin, it is also a world of sorrow.

Indeed, there are many things that bring tears to our eyes which the world knows nothing about such as inward sin, unbelief, anger, rash speech, foolish pride, coldness of heart, lack of resignation to the will of God.

There are even some precious tears shed here that will be dried on the other side of Jordan. Tears of repentance will be no more. Tears of sympathy will not be required. Tears of concern and sadness over lost souls will be ended when we see all things as our Lord sees them. Tears of longing for Christ's presence will all be dried when we are 'forever with the Lord'!

Has not the Lord given us a foretaste of this? Even now, while we live in this world, our heavenly Father does much to dry our tears. The believer's life is not a morbid, sorrow-filled existence. Not at all!

Will There Be Degrees Of Reward In Heaven?

We do have our sorrows. Yet, even in the midst of sorrow our Lord gives us great comfort (Isaiah 43:1-6). He gives us a measure of resignation to his will. He teaches us to trust his providence. He reminds us of his gracious purpose. He causes us to remember his promise. He blesses us with the sense of his presence. He floods our hearts with the knowledge of his love (Ephesians 3:19). He reminds us of the cause of our pain (Hebrews 12:5-12). He causes our hearts to be fixed upon better things (Colossians 3:1-3; 2 Corinthians 4:15-18).

However, in heaven's glory our God will wipe all tears from our eyes. Impossible as it is for us to imagine, there is a time coming when we shall weep no more, and have no cause to weep! Heaven is a place of sure, eternal, ever-increasing bliss; and the cause of that bliss is our God. Heaven is a place of joy without sorrow, laughter without weeping, and pleasantness without pain! In heaven there are no regrets, no remorseful tears, no second thoughts, no lost causes, no sorrows of any kind!

Read this paragraph very carefully. The thoughts expressed here are simply astounding. Though not quoted directly, they are essentially the thoughts expressed by C. H. Spurgeon on this subject. If God did not wipe away all tears from our eyes there would be much weeping in heaven. Our past sins, our unconverted family members forever lost, wasted opportunities, our unkindnesses and lack of love to our brethren here, and the terrible price of our redemption would all cause our hearts to break and our eyes to flow with rivers of tears forever; but it is written, 'God shall wipe away all tears from their eyes; and there shall be no more death, neither sorrow, nor crying, neither shall there be any more pain: for the former things are passed away.' Our great God shall, in heaven's glory, remove us from all sin, remove all sin from us, and remove from us all the consequences of sin. He will remove us from every cause of grief. He will bring us at last into the perfection of complete salvation; and every desire of our hearts will be completely gratified. Then, we will be like Christ. We will be with Christ. We will see Christ. We will love Christ perfectly, serve him unceasingly, worship him without sin, rest in him completely, enjoy him fully, and have him entirely.

Will you be among the blessed company of the redeemed? Will you be with Christ in glory? You will only enter into glory if you are worthy of heaven. You can only be made worthy by the merits of Christ. If you are worthy of everlasting glory you will have all, without degrees, perfectly. Trust Christ and all the glory of Christ in heaven is yours. God help you to trust him.

Will There Be Degrees Of Reward In Heaven?

Ye humble souls, complain no more;
Let faith survey your future store.
How happy, how divinely blest,
The sacred words of truth attest.

In vain the sons of wealth and pride
Despise your lot, your hope deride;
In vain they boast their little stores;
Trifles are theirs, a kingdom yours.

[A kingdom of immense delight,
Where health, and peace, and joy unite;
Where undeclining pleasures rise,
And every wish has full supplies.]

[A kingdom which can ne'er decay,
While time sweeps earthly thrones away;
The state which power and truth sustain,
Unmoved for ever must remain.]

There shall your eyes with rapture view
The glorious Friend that died for you,
That died to ransom, died to raise
To crowns of joy and songs of praise.

Jesus! To thee I breathe my prayer;
Reveal, confirm my interest there;
Whate'er my humble lot below,
This, this my soul desires to know.

Anne Steele

Going Home

For the Lamb which is in the midst of the throne shall feed them, and shall lead them unto living fountains of waters: and God shall wipe away all tears from their eyes.

Revelation 7:17

Chapter 9

No Tears In Heaven

The previous study concluded by showing that among many aspects of our heavenly inheritance with Christ, one thing demonstrates incontrovertibly the equality of the inheritance to all God's elect. There will be no tears in heaven. This subject is so comforting and important that I wish to return to it again. Every believer in this world has many things to make him weep; but in the world to which we are going, there will be no tears. 'For the Lamb which is in the midst of the throne shall feed them, and shall lead them unto living fountains of waters: and God shall wipe away all tears from their eyes.' In this world of sorrow and weeping believers are often found sighing for their heavenly home. A hymn writer wrote,

> Oh, how I long to reach my home,
> My glorious home in heaven!
> And wish the joyful hour were come,
> The welcome mandate given!

Going Home

Oh, how I long to lay aside
These worn out weeds of clay;
And, led by my celestial Guide,
To explore the eternal day!

Oh, how I long to be with Christ,
Where all His glory beams!
To be from all my sin set free,
And worship as I've dreamed!

Oh, how I long to see His smile,
To sit before His feet!
Lord, grant me soon my heart's desire,
Soon, soon Thy work complete.

Charlotte Elliott

Allow me to state my personal thoughts. I neither weary of life, nor weary of serving my Redeemer. The Lord has given me a much fuller and happier life in my years than most men ever have who live twice as long. My heart, mind, and strength are more fully engaged in and zealous for the service of Christ than ever before. Yet, my heart is fixed on better things still. I long to live fully in the presence of Christ. I long to serve my Master perfectly, without sin. This I know, 'to die is gain'. Therefore I have 'a desire to depart and be with Christ, which is far better.'

What does heaven look like? Where is it? How big is heaven? What will we have when we get there? These are the questions about heaven which interest carnal religionists. I hope they are not your primary concern. Still, our minds need some idea of heaven. We need to know something about it. Though much more about heaven is hidden than is revealed, the Lord has revealed as much as we need to know while we are still in our earthly tabernacles of clay.

Heaven is a real place. Our Lord Jesus is there in a real human body (Hebrews 2:9; 10:12-14). All the dead in Christ are there (Hebrews 12:22-24). The angels of God are there, too. Heaven is a place prepared by God and purchased by Christ for God's elect (Matthew 25:34; Hebrews 6:20). It is a place of perfect rest. It is a place of perfect peace. It is a place of perfect love. It is a place of perfect satisfaction. Yet, the fulness, the beauty, and the glory of heaven are things beyond the scope of human understanding or description (2 Corinthians 12:4). Heaven is not a place of carnal sense. It is not a place of human imagination. 'Eye hath not seen, or ear heard, neither have entered into the heart of man, the things which God hath prepared for them that love him' (1 Corinthians 2:9). Your highest, noblest, grandest, most spiritual thoughts about heaven fall far short of its reality. 'Beloved, it doth not yet appear what we shall be' (1 John 3:2). Heaven is not a place of human intellect either, a place discovered, gained, or comprehended by man's genius. The fact is, we do not know what the fulness of heaven shall be. However, of this one thing I am sure, there will be no tears in heaven. It is written, 'God shall wipe away all tears from their eyes.' This is one of the most delightful and comforting aspects of our heavenly inheritance to consider.

Much Weeping

Without question, there is much weeping in the way to heaven. Experimentally, faith in Christ brings deliverance from all curse and condemnation, but as we have seen, not from pain and trouble. There are many things which believers suffer along with other men. God's children in this world experience loss, pain and disappointment. Ask Job and David if these things are not so. The most eminent men of faith and obedience are not exempted from trouble and sorrow in this world. Let no one dupe you into thinking your troubles and sorrows here are an indication of God's disfavour.

In fact, many things bring tears to our eyes concerning which the world knows little. Nothing troubles regenerate souls so much or so persistently as their awareness of their inward sin. Though every saint resigns himself to the rule and will of God his Saviour. Yet, our unceasing lack of resignation is a constant cause of turmoil in our souls. Unbelief, pride, anger, coldness of heart, and fretfulness are but a few of the things every believing heart struggles with daily. Those who know the grace of God have no difficulty understanding Paul's language in Romans 7:14-24. We experience the warfare daily. We know what it is to weep for sin in this world. But when he brings us home, in heaven God will remove all tears from our eyes because heaven is a place of sure, eternal, and ever-increasing bliss. The source of that bliss is God himself.

If God did not wipe away all tears from our eyes, there would be reason for much weeping in heaven. We would never cease to weep over our past sins were it not that the Lord God will then take away the cause of weeping, and show us even our sins were overruled by his gracious and wise hand for our eternal good and his glory. Imagine what such knowledge will be! We would weep forever over unconverted loved ones and friends left behind, were it not that then we shall be fully reconciled to the purpose of God, seeing all things as he sees them. We would weep forever over all the wasted opportunities and time we squandered in this world, did not our Father show us how he has used even our neglect to accomplish his purpose. How we would weep over the great and terrible price of our redemption, if we were not in heaven made to see perfectly the glory of God in the sacrifice of his darling Son. In that world of perfect love, we would weep much over our unkindness and lack of love to our brethren upon the earth, did not our heavenly Father wipe all tears from our eyes.

What a great promise this is that God shall wipe away all tears from our eyes. He will remove every cause of outward grief. He will remove us from all sin and all sin from us. All fear of change shall be shut out. Every desire of our hearts will be gratified. We shall see Christ, be like Christ, love Christ wholly, serve Christ unceasingly, worship Christ without sin, know Christ thoroughly, rest in Christ fully, have Christ entirely, and enjoy Christ completely, perfectly, and eternally!

A Question

Will you be among the happy company of the redeemed? Not everyone will be among the people of God in heaven. No one deserves to be with Christ in heaven. Yet, many will be there. All who were chosen of God in electing love will be there. The purpose of God cannot be thwarted. All who are washed in Christ's blood will be there. The cross of our Lord Jesus Christ shall never fail. The Son of God did not shed his blood in vain. All for whom he endured the travail of the cross, he will see by his side in heaven. All who are clothed with his righteousness will be there. All who love his name will be there. All who believe Christ will be there. God has promised eternal life to all who trust his Son; and he will give what he has promised. 'Dost thou believe on the Son of God?'

Going Home

For I reckon that the sufferings of this present time are not worthy to be compared with the glory which shall be revealed in us. For the earnest expectation of the creature waiteth for the manifestation of the sons of God. For the creature was made subject to vanity, not willingly, but by reason of him who hath subjected the same in hope, Because the creature itself also shall be delivered from the bondage of corruption into the glorious liberty of the children of God. For we know that the whole creation groaneth and travaileth in pain together until now. And not only they, but ourselves also, which have the firstfruits of the Spirit, even we ourselves groan within ourselves, waiting for the adoption, to wit, the redemption of our body.

Romans 8:18-23

Chapter 10

The Magnitude Of Our Heavenly Inheritance

In Romans 8:18-23, as the Apostle Paul discusses the great privileges and prospects of God's elect in Christ, he seems to simply get carried away with the great tide of grace. The greatness of the things he is writing about seems to utterly engulf him. He says, 'If children, then heirs; heirs of God; and joint-heirs with Jesus Christ'! What an inheritance! We possess the inheritance, not by our own rights and merits, but by God's covenant grace and Christ's all-sufficient merit as our Substitute. It is true, we must in this world suffer for a season with him and for his sake; but when our earthly woes are over, we shall reign with him and inherit all things with him as the children of God.

In consideration of these things, the apostle says, 'For I reckon that the sufferings of this present time am not worthy to be compared with the glory which shall be revealed in us.' This 'glory which shall be revealed in us' is not the glory that will be ours as soon as we die and enter into heaven with Christ. This is more. It is the glory that will be ours in the consummation of our salvation at the resurrection. It is something indescribable even by one who was inspired by God. Paul seems to search for words to speak of it. Notice, just in these few verses, he calls it four different things.

1. 'The glory which shall be revealed in us' (v. 18).
2. 'The manifestation of the sons of God' (v. 19).
3. 'The glorious liberty of the sons of God' (v. 21).
4. 'The redemption of our body' (v. 23).

This is the 'blessed hope and glorious appearing of the great God and our Saviour' (Titus 2:13) for which we are to look constantly. This is that for which Peter admonishes us to, 'Gird up the loins of our minds, and be sober, and hope to the end for the grace that is to be brought unto us at the revelation of Jesus Christ' (1 Peter 1:13). This heavenly inheritance is an inheritance of indescribable, universal greatness and glory.

No Comparison
The glory to be revealed in us is of such magnitude that the sufferings of this present time are not worthy to be compared to it. Paul writes, in verse eighteen, 'For I reckon that the sufferings of this present time are not worthy to be compared with the glory which shall be revealed in us.' The Apostle Paul uses a kind of spiritual arithmetic here. He places these two opposite things in two separate columns. The amount of our sufferings in this world, he acknowledges to be very great. In the other column, he sees the amount of glory that is to be revealed in us, and says, 'the sufferings of this present time are not worthy to even be put in the scales with the glory that shall be revealed in us.'

The Magnitude Of Our Heavenly Inheritance

The sufferings of this present time are, for many of God's saints, great. I know that compared to what Christ suffered for us, compared to what so many others have and do suffer in this world, compared to what we deserve, and compared to the glory awaiting us, our sorrows here are but 'light afflictions'. However, I do not suggest that you try telling a man who has just buried his only child that his affliction is light. The misery of man in this world is great upon him. Viewed in themselves, our woes are hard to bear, heavy, and painful beyond description. We all know some people who carry heavy, heavy burdens. Yet, the heaviest of our temporary, earthly burdens and woes are not worthy to be compared to the glory that shall be revealed in us.

We should always try to remember our sufferings are confined to this present time. The short duration of any agony makes it bearable, when we are confident the agony will be succeeded by a long time of relief and enjoyment. Jacob's fourteen years of service to Laban for Rachel seemed to him but a few days because of the love he had for her (Genesis 29:20). A mother's travail in birth is forgotten as soon as her baby is in her arms. Our Lord Jesus was sustained in his agony of body, heart, and soul by the joyful prospect of having his ransomed ones with him in heaven (Hebrews 12:2). So, too, our hearts are sustained in trouble when we look beyond present things to eternal things (2 Corinthians 4:17-5:1).

The glory of the heavenly inheritance awaiting us will be so magnificently great it will remove from us every painful memory of sorrow in this world. Indeed, our sorrows here will only add to the glory of the world to come. I cannot tell you how, but I know when we have entered into our glory, our happiness and glory in eternity will be greater because of our sorrows here. 'For our light affliction, which is but for a moment, worketh for us a far more exceeding and eternal weight of glory.' 'Wherein ye greatly rejoice, though now for a season, if need be, ye are in heaviness through manifold temptations: That the trial of your faith, being much more precious than of gold that perisheth, though it be tried with fire, might be found unto praise and honour and glory at the appearing of Jesus Christ' (2 Corinthians 4:17; 1 Peter 1:6, 7).

'Such will be the joy of the heavenly inheritance,' an old preacher said, 'that it will efface from our remembrance the few years of sorrow which have preceded it; so efface them, at least, that we shall never think of them with regret, but as a foil to heighten our bliss.' The sufferings of this present time, therefore, are not worthy to be compared to that glory that shall be revealed in us.

Influence And Effects
The glory to be revealed in us at the resurrection is so great and marvellous it influences and affects the whole of God's creation.

> For the earnest expectation of the creature waiteth for the manifestation of the sons of God. For the creature was made subject to vanity, not willingly, but by reason of him who hath subjected the same in hope, Because the creature itself also shall be delivered from the bondage of corruption into the glorious liberty of the children of God. For we know that the whole creation groaneth and travaileth in pain together until now (vv. 19-22).

The creature, that is to say, the whole creation of God was brought into bondage by the sin and fall of our father Adam. Adam's sin reached beyond the human race. It affected the whole earth. The whole creation was brought into the bondage of corruption, not willingly, but in consequence of Adam's transgression. The ground itself was cursed. Adam's house cat became a roaring lion and his dog a ravening wolf. This subjection of the creation to the bondage of corruption was by the hand of God; but it was not to be permanent. God 'subjected the same in hope'. This simply means that when we are delivered from the curse of sin, God's creation will also be delivered from the bondage of corruption. The redemption of our bodies in the resurrection will be the birthday of a new creation. Because of Adam's sin everything in God's earthly creation has become in some way subservient to evil; but God will not allow this state of affairs to continue. He will, when he completes our redemption, completely restore his creation to himself, so everything shall serve and praise him. There is a day appointed when there will be a restitution of all things to God (Acts 3:21; Ephesians 1:9, 10).

When the Lord God created the heavens and the earth in their pristine form, everything, according to its nature and capacity, displayed his glory. To a very great extent they still do (Psalm 19:1-4). This was the natural order of things by God's design. Either consciously or unconsciously, everything furnished its tribute of praise to him who is over all God blessed forever. The entrance of sin into the world changed everything. Everything God created for the comfort of man has been abused by man. Everything God gave us to use in serving him and honouring him, we have sacrificed to Baal (Hosea 2:8). Everything in the world has been sacrificed to some imaginary deity or idolatrous thought. Every benefit of creation has been employed by us to serve and gratify our lusts. The creation itself has been turned into a god to be worshipped! The earth is called, 'Mother Earth'! Nature is called, 'Mother Nature'! Even time is worshipped as, 'Father Time'. Nature, with fallen man, occupies the place of God. We have 'changed the truth of God into a lie, and worshipped and served the creature more than the Creator, who is blessed for ever' (Romans 1:25).

Though the creatures have no reason or intelligence, yet there is, as it were, such an instinctive tendency in God's creation to oppose man that the whole of creation is at war with fallen man. Were that not the case, there would be no reason for a covenant to be made on our behalf with the beasts of the field, the fowls of the air, the creeping things of the earth, and the very stones of the ground (Hosea 2:18). The Holy Spirit assures us this bondage of God's creation is only temporary. God, in his infinite wisdom, saw fit to subject the creation to the bondage of corruption for a season. However, it is specifically said to be a subjection 'in hope' because there is a time set by God when he will deliver his creation from the bondage of corruption. The redemption of our bodies from the grave will be for us the destruction of our last enemy and the termination of all the effects of sin. It will also be the termination of bondage and corruption, of all the corrupting effects of sin, upon God's creation. It is for this the whole creation groans and travails.

Notice again the fourfold description given of our heavenly inheritance (Romans 8:18-23). As we look at these descriptions of glory, remember Paul is talking about the perfecting and completing of our salvation through the death of Christ, which is the greatest possible display of the glory of God. This will be the last of the great series of events God has been performing from the beginning of time. This is the thing for which all things were made and to which all things are subjected. This glorious inheritance is the goal of election and predestination and the object of providence (Romans 8:28-30; Ephesians 1:3-6). First, it is called, 'the glory that shall be revealed in us'. This refers to the manifestation of God's glory that shall be revealed in our consummate salvation (Ephesians 1:6, 12, 14; 2:7). Second, the completion of God's work of grace is called, 'the manifestation of the sons of God'. Here, God's saints are little known and hardly noticed, except when derided by the wicked; but there is

118

a day coming which will be the day of our manifestation (1 John 3:1, 2). Third, our ultimate salvation is described as 'the glorious liberty of the sons of God'. This will be our happy jubilee! When it comes, we shall be freed from the penalty and dominion of sin. At death, we shall be delivered from the presence of sin; but when Christ comes, when the jubilee trumpet sounds, we shall be delivered from all the consequences of sin. Fourth, we shall experience, 'the redemption of our body'. We will sing the song of triumph and victory as we look back upon our empty graves, 'O death, where is thy sting? O grave, where is thy victory? The sting of death is sin; and the strength of sin is the law. But thanks be to God, which giveth us the victory through our Lord Jesus Christ' (1 Corinthians 15:55-57).

Our Groaning

Such is the magnitude, greatness, grandeur, and glory of our heavenly inheritance that our highest and greatest enjoyments in this world can never satisfy us. We groan within ourselves, waiting for the redemption of our body. 'And not only they, but ourselves also, which have the firstfruits of the Spirit, even we ourselves groan within ourselves, waiting for the adoption, to wit, the redemption of our body' (v. 23).

First, the apostle says that we who have the firstfruits of the Spirit groan within ourselves. These are the groanings spoken of in verse 26. Firstfruits are delightful, but never satisfying. We groan for the full harvest (Romans 7:24).

Second, Paul speaks of us waiting for our adoption. We were adopted into the family of God by divine decree in eternal election (Ephesians 1:3-6). We were experimentally adopted into the family of God in regeneration when we received the Spirit of adoption (Galatians 4:6, 7). We shall enter into the full enjoyment of our adoption in the resurrection.

Third, the apostle describes our resurrection, our entrance into heavenly inheritance with Christ, as 'the redemption of our body'. Christ is made Redemption (1 Corinthians 1:30) unto us in a threefold sense.

1. We were redeemed from the curse of the law and penalty of sin by the ransom price of Christ's shed blood when he died as our Substitute (Galatians 3:13).

2. We were redeemed from the rule and dominion of sin by the power of God's grace in regeneration (Romans 6:18).

3. We shall be redeemed from all the consequences of sin in the resurrection.

What a glorious hope is set before us? Let us set our hearts upon it (Colossians 3:1-3).

This great, glorious, indescribably majestic inheritance shall be the glorious consummation of Christ's reign as our King (1 Corinthians 15:24-28). It is this blessed hope which fills believing hearts with expectant anticipation in this world.

The Magnitude Of Our Heavenly Inheritance

Yes, I shall soon be landed
On yonder shores of bliss;
There, with my powers expanded,
Shall dwell where Jesus is.

Yes, I shall soon be seated,
With Jesus on his throne,
My foes be all defeated,
And sacred peace made known.

With Father, Son and Spirit,
I shall for ever reign,
Sweet joy and peace inherit,
And every good obtain.

I soon shall reach the harbour,
To which I speed my way,
Shall cease from all my labour,
And there for ever stay.

Sweet Spirit, guide me over
This life's tempestuous sea;
Keep me, O holy Lover,
For I confide in thee.

Oh, that in Jordan's swelling
I may be helped to sing,
And pass the river telling
The triumphs of my King.

Gospel Magazine, 1804

Going Home

And he shewed me a pure river of water of life, clear as crystal, proceeding out of the throne of God and of the Lamb. In the midst of the street of it, and on either side of the river, was there the tree of life, which bare twelve manner of fruits, and yielded her fruit every month: and the leaves of the tree were for the healing of the nations. And there shall be no more curse: but the throne of God and of the Lamb shall be in it; and his servants shall serve him: And they shall see his face; and his name shall be in their foreheads. And there shall be no night there; and they need no candle, neither light of the sun; for the Lord God giveth them light: and they shall reign for ever and ever.

Revelation 22:1-5

Chapter 11

With Christ In Heaven: Paradise Regained

When God created the first man, Adam, he placed him in the Garden of Eden. Eden was a place of innocence, abundance, life and joy. It was paradise on earth; but paradise was not complete for Adam until the Lord God gave him a woman to be his bride. The Lord caused Adam to sleep in the earth and took a rib from his side. From Adam's wounded side, Eve was made. She came from Adam. She was a part of Adam. Without Adam, Eve could never have lived. Yet, without Eve, Adam could never have been complete.

Adam and Eve had for their home the paradise of God. There they lived in perfect harmony, holiness, and happiness until the serpent beguiled Eve and persuaded her to eat of the tree of the knowledge of good and evil. When Adam saw what Eve had done, he took the fruit of the tree in rebellion against God. Sin had entered the world. Paradise was lost. Fallen man was driven away from the presence of the Lord.

In the fulness of time, the second Adam, the last Adam, was born. Jesus Christ, the Son of God, came into the world to seek his beloved Bride, his elect Church. He came to recover for us what we lost in Adam. By his obedience unto death, he has regained for us everything we lost in Adam: righteousness, peace, life, fellowship with God, and paradise. He has already entered the paradise of God as our representative, claiming it in the name of his people (Hebrews 6:20). Yet, as Adam without Eve was incomplete, so Christ without his beloved Bride is incomplete. The Head must have the Body. The Bridegroom must have his Bride. Christ must have his Church, 'Which is his body, the fulness of him that filleth all in all' (Ephesians 1:23). When Christ and his Church are united in heaven, in the perfection of heavenly glory, paradise shall be fully recovered.

In Revelation 22:1-5, John describes the Holy City, New Jerusalem, using symbols drawn from the Garden of Eden. The eternal, heavenly state of God's saints with Christ is paradise regained. Our Lord said to the thief on the cross, 'Today shalt thou be with me in paradise' (Luke 23:43). The apostle Paul was 'caught up into paradise' (2 Corinthians 12:4). That blessed place and condition is described as, 'The paradise of God' (Revelation 2:7). When God's saints leave this world, they enter into paradise, not purgatory, not limbo, but paradise. What is it like? In these five verses John shows us six things about paradise:

1. The River Of Paradise
The earthly paradise was watered by a mighty river; but it was only a river of water for the earth. The heavenly paradise is watered by the river of the water of life (v. 1). This river of the water of life is the everlasting love of God (Psalm 46:4). Like a river, the love of God is ever-flowing towards his elect, it is abundant and free (Ephesians 3:18, 19). The streams of this river make glad the hearts of God's

people. The streams of this river, like the river in Eden, run in four directions across the earth. The streams of the river are: eternal election, blood atonement, effectual calling, peace, pardon, justification, and eternal life. Flowing, as they do, to sinners from the river of God's everlasting love, through the mediation of Christ, these blessings of grace bring us eternal life. This river is called the 'river of the water of life' (Zechariah 14:8, 9; John 7:38, 39), and because the love of God is the source and cause of life, it revives the saints with life, and sustains them in life.

God's love for us is a mighty, flowing river that is pure and clear as crystal. His love for us is pure, sincere, true, and without hypocrisy. It is as clear as crystal. It is free, without motive or condition. It promotes purity. The gospel, which reveals it, is a gospel of purity and holiness. The grace which is the fruit of it is righteousness. Every discovery of this love compels and constrains us to consecrate ourselves to Christ in obedience, love and faith. The love of God is free of licentiousness and can never promote licentiousness.

The source of this great river of love is the throne of God and of the Lamb. God's love for us is not caused by or conditioned upon our obedience or love to him. His love for us precedes our love for him and is the cause of our love for him (1 John 4:19). God's love for us is not caused or conditioned even upon the obedience and death of Christ as our Substitute. It was God's love for us that sent Christ to die for us and redeem us (John 3:16; Romans 5:8; 1 John 3:16; 4:9, 10). God's love for his elect is free. He said, from eternity, 'I will love them freely' (Hosea 14:4). God's love for us is like God himself, it is eternal, immutable, and indestructible. The source and cause of his love is his own sovereign will and pleasure (Romans 9:11-18). It cannot be attributed to anything else.

2. The Tree Of Paradise

In the Garden of Eden there was a tree of life. Adam, by sin, lost his right to eat of that tree. In the paradise of God there is another Tree of Life. That Tree of Life is the Lord Jesus Christ himself. He is that One in heaven who heals chosen sinners scattered throughout the nations of the earth by virtue of his finished work of redemption and by the power of his Holy Spirit. Christ, the Tree of Life, fills heaven. He is seen in the midst of the street and on both sides of the river. The City of God is full of Christ. That is the blessedness of heaven. Christ is there! Luther's doctrine concerning the ubiquity of Christ's physical body after his glorification may not be correct, but his heavenly body is such that he is immediately known and accessible everywhere and to everyone at all times. What mortal can imagine such a body? Our Saviour's immortal body and the immortal bodies we shall have after the resurrection will be free of all limitations and hindrances necessary to this earthly existence. Christ, the Tree of Life, bears twelve manner of fruits. He bears fruit for the twelve tribes of the Israel of God. He has fruit sufficient for the whole Israel of God, the whole body of his elect. All fulness is in him and we have our perfection and completion in him (John 1:16; Ephesians 1:6; Colossians 2:9). The fruit of this Tree of Life is abundant at all times. From it we obtain abundant, perfect righteousness, sufficient both for justification and for sanctification; plenteous redemption, from the curse of the law by Christ's atonement, from the dominion of sin by the power of his grace, and from the very being and consequences of sin by the resurrection of our bodies; and eternal life, with all its blessedness in time and eternity. The leaves of this Tree are for the healing of the nations. The leaves of this Tree are the blessed gospel doctrines of substitutionary redemption and imputed righteousness. Through the preaching of the gospel today, God sends his grace into the nations of the world for the healing of men's souls (Romans 1:15, 16; 10:17; 1 Corinthians 1:21). And in heaven's glory, the leaves of this tree, the blessed gospel of Christ, will yet preserve all God's elect in life as the tree of life in Eden would have preserved Adam in life had he continued there (Genesis 3:22-24). Even in that blessed, eternal state God's saints will be 'kept by the power of his grace'. In a word, everything in Christ will unceasingly contribute to and secure the everlasting life and joy of God's saints in heaven.

3. The Freedom Of Paradise

'And there shall be no more curse.' Having been redeemed from the curse of the law by Christ's precious blood (Galatians 3:13), the curse of the law cannot fall upon the redeemed. Where there is no sin, there is no cause for the curse. The Lord Jesus Christ has put away our sins forever. We shall not even suffer loss or be treated any the less graciously because of our sin. God will not impute sin to those for whom Christ has died (Romans 4:8), neither in this world, nor in the world to come. In that blessed state awaiting us there shall be no possibility of a curse because there shall be no possibility of sin. Not only has the Son of God saved us from the fall, he has saved us from the possibility of another fall (John 10:28). Consequently, in the holy city, New Jerusalem, there will never even be the fear of the curse of God's holy law!

4. The Throne Of Paradise

'But the throne of God and of the Lamb shall be in it.' It is the presence and stability of this throne that guarantees the security of God's saints and removes all possibility of curse from us. It is called 'the throne of God and of the Lamb' because God and the Lamb are One and God is seen, known, and revealed only in the Lamb (John 1:14, 18). This throne is the source of all things, the rule of all things, and the end of all things (Romans 11:36). This throne is the joy of all believers and the dread of all rebels. It is a throne of free grace (Hebrews 4:16) and sovereign dominion (Daniel 4:35-37).

5. The Joy Of Paradise

'His servants shall serve him.' In eternity we will serve God our Saviour perfectly and perpetually.

'And they shall see his face.' Then, when we see him face to face who loved us and gave himself for us, we shall enjoy perfect communion with him, complete acceptance with God in him and with him, and full satisfaction in him. In heaven's glory he will make a full disclosure of himself, his works, and his ways to us. And when we see his face, seeing all things as he sees them, we will be filled with intense, indescribable delight!

'And his name shall be in their foreheads.' That simply means we will own and be owned, accept and be accepted of our God forever. We will confess him to be our God; and he will confess us to be his people forever.

'And there shall be no night there.' There will be no darkness of any kind in heaven: no darkness of sin, sorrow, ignorance, or bigotry. In the New Jerusalem there will be no need for secondary lights, no need for the symbolic ordinances that now contribute so much to our worship, neither believer's baptism signifying the confession of Christ, nor the Lord's Supper signifying the remembrance of Christ. There will not even be a need of pastors and teachers to instruct, guide, and correct us. The reason is simple, 'For the Lord God giveth them light.'

6. The Duration Of Paradise

'And they shall reign for ever and ever.' When the Lord Jesus Christ has presented his Bride, his body, the church and kingdom of God in its entirety to the Father; when he has presented us holy, blameless, unreproveable, and glorious, we shall reign with him for ever and ever (1 Corinthians 15:24-28) in 'the glorious liberty of the children of God' (Romans 8:21). Let these thoughts sustain, comfort, and rejoice your heart, child of God, as you live in the hope of that city whose Builder and Maker is your God.

Our Adam, the last Adam, the Lord Jesus Christ is in paradise now. From his wounded side, God is forming a bride for him. Paradise will not be complete for Christ until he has his beloved Bride with him. And Christ shall have his bride. Not one of God's elect, given to Christ in eternity, redeemed by Christ at Calvary, and called by the Spirit of Christ in time shall be missing in the heavenly paradise.

Going Home

Fear and dread shall fall upon them; by the greatness of thine arm they shall be as still as a stone; till thy people pass over, O LORD, till the people pass over, which thou hast purchased. Thou shalt bring them in, and plant them in the mountain of thine inheritance, in the place, O LORD, which thou hast made for thee to dwell in, in the Sanctuary, O Lord, which thy hands have established. The LORD shall reign for ever and ever.

Exodus 15:16-18

Chapter 12

The Believer's Easy Passage Through Death To Glory

I have seen people die without Christ, without faith in him, and without hope. I have seen the terror of hell on their helpless, hopeless faces as they gasped for their last breath of life. I pray I will never see that pitiful expression again. However, I have also seen some of God's saints die in faith, with the smile of God upon their souls and the peace of God radiating through their words. I cannot imagine a more delightful or more glorious thing to behold on this earth. Balaam spoke well when he said, 'Let me die the death of the righteous, and let my last end be like his' (Numbers 23:10).

Exodus chapter 15 records Moses' song of redemption and salvation. In verses 1-13 he sang praise to God for the redemption, grace and salvation Israel had just experienced. In verses 14-19 he praises God for the sure hope of a peaceful and glorious entrance into the land of promise. Specifically, in verses 16-18, the prophet of God speaks of the safe, peaceful passage of Israel across the Jordan river into the land of Canaan. This prophetical song was written for us. Typically, prophetically, it declares how God's saints will pass through death into glory safely and peacefully, by the greatness of his arm. 'Fear and dread shall fall upon them; by the greatness of thine arm they shall be as still as a stone; till thy people pass over, O LORD, till the people pass over, which thou hast purchased. Thou shalt bring them in, and plant them in the mountain of thine inheritance, in the place, O LORD, which thou hast made for thee to dwell in, in the Sanctuary, O Lord, which thy hands have established. The LORD shall reign for ever and ever.' Viewing these words as a picture of every believer's easy passage through death into heaven, they teach us four great spiritual truths.

A Purchased People

The Lord Jesus Christ has a people in this world whom he has purchased. Moses spoke of the Lord's people as those whom he has purchased. Who are these people? They are the people of God's choice, his peculiar people. These purchased people are those men and women with whom Christ's delights were from everlasting. They are peculiarly and distinctively his (Deuteronomy 7:7-9). They are chosen in electing love (John 15:16). They are redeemed by his precious blood (1 Peter 1:18). They are called by almighty grace (Psalm 65:4). They are given faith in Christ by the operation of his Spirit (Colossians 2:12). If you are a believer, you are one of his people whom he has purchased!

Christ alone is the Purchaser of his people. He alone was able and willing to do it, as the God-man, our Mediator. He alone has the lawful right to do it, as our Kinsman Redeemer. He alone has done it. Christ did not try to redeem anyone, or merely make redemption available for everyone. He effectually redeemed all his people by his sin-atoning sacrifice at Calvary (Galatians 3:13; Hebrews 9:12).

The Believer's Easy Passage Through Death To Glory

When the Word of God talks about redemption, it is talking about something that is finished (Daniel 9:24; John 19:30.) The thing is done, not provided, but done. 'Thou hast purchased'! 'Ye are bought with a price'! (1 Corinthians 6:20). The price by which the Son of God purchased his people is his own precious blood (1 Peter 1:18, 19; Revelation 5:9; Acts 20:28). How this glorious subject ought to thrill our souls! The redemption accomplished by Christ at Calvary was a special purchase. He has purchased a special people, with a special price, because of special love, to enjoy special blessings of grace and glory forever. It was a proper purchase. We sometimes use the words 'buy' or 'purchase' in other ways (Isaiah 55:1). We purchase grace and mercy, without money and without price, by faith in Christ. That is not the case here. Christ made a real, proper purchase of God's elect by the price of his own blood. It was a legal purchase (Isaiah 43:1). The people were named. He died for and purchased 'his people' (Isaiah 53:8; John 10:11, 15, 26). The price was agreed to (Romans 3:24-26). The purchase was made (Romans 5:8-11). It cannot be invalidated (Romans 11:29). It is a full and complete purchase. Here is the greatest purchase ever made. Christ has redeemed and purchased a great multitude which no man can number, who could not be redeemed by any other price than his precious blood (Psalm 49:7, 8; Job 36:18). We rejoice to know Christ has a people in this world whom he has purchased.

Nothing so comforts dying saints as the knowledge of effectually accomplished redemption by the blood of Christ. Several years ago, I visited a dying friend. His last words to me, as I started to leave him were, 'Brother, my hope is in that Man in heaven whose blood has washed away all of my sins and given me perfect righteousness before God. Thank God for Christ. I thank God for the blood of Christ! I am thankful to know there is a Man in glory who is my Substitute. My hope is him!' Our hearts are overwhelmed with joy to know we are among those people for whom redemption is accomplished. I say, with my brother, 'Thank God for Christ! Thank God for the blood of Christ!'

Pass Through Death

Though redeemed by blood and saved by grace, God's purchased people must pass through death into glory. As Israel must pass through the Jordan River to reach the land of Canaan, so God's pilgrims in this world must pass through death to reach their home in glory. Notice two things in this regard.

1. Death For The Believer Is Just A Passage

Death is passing from this world to another world, from time into eternity. It is to depart from this world and be with Christ, which is far better (Philippians 1:23). It is a passage through a low, lonesome valley (Psalm 23:4). But do not let that prospect frighten you. This life is the valley of the shadow of death. The Puritan, Thomas Brooks, wrote, 'Death to a saint is nothing but the taking of a sweet flower out of this wilderness, and planting it in the garden of paradise.' Moses compared death to passing over a river, crossing from this shore to that shore. For the believer that is all death is, a passage from this foreign, condemned land to our homeland in glory!

2. It Is A Necessary Passage

Death must be. This is the way of all the earth. There is no avoiding it. The grave is the house appointed for all living. Your grave may be a stately mausoleum or a pit in the earth; but to the grave you must go, and so must I, at the time appointed of God (Hebrews 9:27; Job 30:23; Genesis 47:29). Just as 'the time drew nigh that Israel must die,' so the time draws near when each of us must die. There was no other way for Israel to get to Canaan, but by going through Jordan, so there is no other way for us to go to heaven but by the grave. Even Enoch and Elijah, though they escaped death, did not escape the change all must undergo before we can enter glory. Even those saints living at Christ's second advent must be changed. Someone said, 'Were it not for sin, death had never had a beginning, and were it not for death, sin would never have had an ending.' We must die. Yet, in reality, the believer never dies (John 11:25). Christ has taken the sting out of death for us. He has delivered us from death's penal aspect. He has delivered us from the second death. Soon, he will deliver every believer from sin and all the consequences of sin. We ought never to look upon that deliverance as death. At death, we begin to live!

We may not presently think so, but for the dying believer, death is a friend, a welcome, long-expected friend, who brings with him great relief and comfort. It is necessary because of sin. It is welcome because of grace. This body of flesh is our greatest enemy. Death will be a welcome relief.

Safe And Peaceful
The believer's passage through death into glory is always safe and usually peaceful. My primary reason for writing these studies is to assure the children of God there is nothing in death that should cause them fear, either for themselves or for their departed friends and loved ones who sleep in their Saviour's arms. When Joshua and the children of Israel came to the river Jordan and passed over it, not one was lost, missing, or hurt by it. It shall be so with God's elect. Every one of the Lord's purchased people shall pass through the Jordan and come safe at last into the heavenly Canaan. You who were ordained to eternal life shall possess it. You who have been purchased by Christ's blood shall see the Lamb for sinners slain. You who are united to Christ shall be with Christ in glory. You who have the earnest of the Spirit shall have the full inheritance of glory. You who

have faith in Christ shall be found with Christ. You who are under Christ's care and in his hands shall be presented by Christ to your heavenly Father (Hebrews 2:13). You to whom God has given grace, will be given glory also. As Israel lost nothing by passing from the wilderness through Jordan into Canaan, so God's saints lose nothing by passing through death into glory. They go immediately into heaven (2 Corinthians 5:1-4, 8). As we have seen, all their most earnest and constant prayers are answered in an instant. They shall be first in the resurrection (1 Thessalonians 4:16).

Moreover, generally speaking, God's saints pass through death into glory peaceably, with quiet, comfortable confidence. I do not say that every believer will be absolutely free of fear and trouble in the hour of death; but generally they are. I do not suggest we are freed from the fear of death as we think about it. Yet, I do say, generally, when a believer is faced with death, he is filled with peace. God does not give dying grace until it is needed. However, when it is needed, he does not fail to give it. In that hour your enemies shall be 'as still as a stone'.

When Israel went out of Egypt, not a dog was allowed to move its tongue against them. No enemy molested them. No foe gave them any disturbance. They left Egypt with a high hand, triumphantly! When they passed over Jordan into the land of Canaan, though they had many enemies, not one was to be seen or heard. They were all, as Moses said, 'As still as a stone', until God's people had passed over. So it is with God's saints in the hour of death. As a general rule, those spiritual enemies who have given you so much uneasiness in life, will not be allowed to distress you in your last moments on this earth.

Your inward sins and corruptions of nature will not be able to rob you of peace either, when certain deliverance is at hand. John Gill said, 'The believer perceiving his dissolution drawing nigh, spies deliverance from it through Jesus Christ our Lord' (Romans 7:23-25). This confidence and peace arises from 'a comfortable view of the free and full forgiveness of his sins through the blood of Christ; and of his justification before God, and acceptance with him through his pure and perfect righteousness.' Thomas Watson wrote, 'He may look upon death with joy who can look on forgiveness with faith.' When the Puritan Thomas Goodwin was on his death bed, in his dying hour, he referred to his inward sins as 'croaking toads', and said, 'Thank God, in a short time I will hear no more their croaking language'!

An evil heart of unbelief will not likely distress the soul that is about to leave the realm of unbelief forever. Nothing makes God's children more uneasy in life than an evil heart of unbelief; but in the hour of death, God graciously drives this monster from the hearts of his children, even as he did with David (2 Samuel 23:5) and Paul (2 Timothy 1:12; 4:6-8). It is written of God's saints, 'These all died in faith' (Hebrews 11:13), because 'the righteous hath hope in his death' (Proverbs 14:32). When he knew he was dying, God's faithful servant, John Gill, said to a friend standing by, 'I have nothing to make me uneasy.'

Your adversary the devil will find it hard to overwhelm you when you are about to tread him beneath your feet (Romans 16:20). Satan is a very busy adversary. His temptations are many and great. In the hour of death, I am sure, he will come against us with all his force like a flood; but our Comforter, the Spirit of God, will lift up a banner against him and put him to flight (Isaiah 59:19). The banner he shall lift to defend us is the gospel of Christ; his Person, his blood, his intercession, and his righteousness. I do not doubt that believing saints, as they leave this world and soar through the heavens into glory crying, 'O Death, where is thy sting?', do so with the same bold challenges raised by the Apostle in Romans 8, 'If God be for us, who can be against us?' 'Who shall lay anything to the charge of God's elect?' 'Who is he that condemneth?' 'Who shall separate us from the love of Christ?' (Romans 8:32-39). 'Mark the perfect man, and behold the upright: for the end of that man is peace' (Psalm 37:37; compare 1 Corinthians 15:55-57).

God's Mighty Arm

This safe and peaceful passage of God's saints through death into glory must be ascribed to the greatness of his arm.

> Fear and dread shall fall upon them; by the greatness of thine arm they shall be as still as a stone; till thy people pass over, O LORD, till the people pass over, which thou hast purchased. Thou shalt bring them in and plant them in the mountain of thine inheritance, in the place, O LORD, which thou hast made for thee to dwell in, in the Sanctuary, O Lord, which thy hands have established. The LORD shall reign for ever and ever.
>
> Exodus 15:16-18

Read Joshua the third chapter. There we find many things by which God made Israel's passage through Jordan into Canaan comfortable and peaceful. These are the very things that will make our passage out of this world into heaven comfortable and peaceful.

1. The presence of the Lord sustained them (Joshua 3:10; Psalm 23:4).
2. The ark of the Lord, the symbol of accomplished redemption, of satisfied justice, of blood atonement, went before them (v. 11).
3. The priests of God led the way, even as Christ has gone into heaven, leading the way before us (Joshua 3:11; Hebrews 6:20).

4. As the priests stood firm upon dry ground (Joshua 3:17), so God's faithful servants, standing firm upon the gospel, inspire God's saints with confident hope of eternal life in and by Christ (Hebrews 13:7, 8).

5. The sight of the waters divided before them (Joshua 3:13) was a picture of salvation accomplished by the hand of God.

With this confidence of faith, we may well die in peace. Our passage through death into heaven will be both safe and easy, being assured that Christ will have his purchased people.

> And an highway shall be there, and a way, and it shall be called The way of holiness; the unclean shall not pass over it; but it shall be for those: the wayfaring men, though fools, shall not err therein. No lion shall be there, nor any ravenous beast shall go up thereon, it shall not be found there; but the redeemed shall walk there: And the ransomed of the LORD shall return, and come to Zion with songs and everlasting joy upon their heads: they shall obtain joy and gladness, and sorrow and sighing shall flee away (Isaiah 35:8-10).

Going Home

And there shall in no wise enter into it any thing that defileth, neither whatsoever worketh abomination, or maketh a lie: but they which are written in the Lamb's book of life.

Revelation 21:27

Chapter 13

Heaven: Who Shall Enter In?

The church of God in this world is like the tabernacle in the wilderness. Within it is lit up with the glory of God's presence. We are the temple of the living God. God dwells in our midst. God the Holy Spirit resides in the hearts of his people. And the one Person who always attends the assembly of the saints is the Son of God, our Saviour, the Lord Jesus Christ. Wherever two or three gather in his name, he is present with them (Matthew 18:20). To gather as a church in the name of Christ means much more than merely wearing his name, saying his name, or claiming the authority of his name. Those who gather in Christ's name come together trusting his name, trusting his blood and righteousness as their only acceptance with the holy Lord God. They come together for the worship of his name, calling upon him in adoration, prayer, praise, and faith. To gather in his name is to gather for the glory of his name, with the intent of making his name known.

Without, God's church is guided and protected by the fiery and cloudy pillar of God's eternal providence. As God led Israel in the wilderness, fed them, protected them, and defended them under the symbol of the fiery and cloudy pillar, so he leads, feeds, protects, and defends his church today.

Yet, outwardly, to all outward appearance, the church of God in this world is a common, unattractive, despised thing. Insofar as the nations were concerned the tabernacle was nothing but a crude tent. God was there, but they knew it not. The altar was there, but they had no use for it. The sacrifice of atonement was there but they despised it. The mercy-seat was there, but they could not see it. All they could see was a poor, homeless people, who had no place to worship but a crude tent, and a people who claimed to be the only true worshippers of God in the world. Faithful Israelites would not worship at any other altar. They refused to acknowledge as brethren any who would not worship their God. They acknowledged one way of salvation only, blood! For these things, they were always despised, persecuted, and mocked by the world around them.

The tabernacle in the wilderness was, in these ways, a symbol and picture of God's church in this world. God dwells in his church. Christ Jesus guides and protects his church. But the world, and all the religions of the world, mock and despise the church of God. That shall not always be the case.

There is a day coming when the tables will be turned. In the last day, the Lord God will reveal his glory in his church and glorify his church before all the universe (John 17:22, 23; Ephesians 2:7). In Revelation 21:10-27, John shows us the glorified church of God in the last day. Paul speaks of the same thing in Ephesians 5:25-27. Christ loved his church. He died to redeem his church. He sanctifies his church. He will perfect and glorify his church. And in the last day, the Lord Jesus will present his church, in all the resurrection glory he puts upon her, to the Father's throne. Then all the world shall marvel at the glory and grace of God in Christ bestowed upon and revealed in his church.

Study John's description of her glory. We shall be presented before the throne of God, before the adoring angels, before Satan, and before the eyes of the damned as a virgin bride (v. 9), the city of God (vv. 10, 11), a walled fortress (v. 12), a great, massive city (vv. 12-17), a perfect, complete city (v. 16), an indescribably wealthy people (vv. 18-21), a perfectly happy, satisfied people (vv. 22, 23), a universally honoured, glorious church (vv. 24-26).

The church of God shall be the crowning glory of the new creation in eternity. 'As it is written, Eye hath not seen, nor ear heard, neither have entered into the heart of man, the things which God hath prepared for them that love him' (1 Corinthians 2:9). No tongue can tell, because no mind can conceive the glory that awaits the church of God in heaven's eternal bliss. Write my name among these blessed ones. My soul thirsts for the living God and the glory that awaits his church in heaven. To dwell in the presence of Christ, to be where he is, to be like he is, to behold his glory, this is the very heaven of heaven!

Yet some will never enter into the glory and bliss of heaven. It is written, in verse twenty-seven, 'And there shall in no wise enter into it anything that defileth, neither whatsoever worketh abomination, or maketh a lie: but they which are written in the Lamb's book of life.' Heaven is an eternal estate of perfect holiness into which nothing but perfect holiness can enter.

A Solemn Fact
Here is a very solemn fact. 'There shall in no wise enter into it anything that defileth, neither whatsoever worketh abomination, or maketh a lie.' Heaven will never be polluted by sin. Almighty God is

holy, righteous, just, and perfect. That which dwells with him forever must be holy, righteous, just and perfect. In order for anything, or anyone, to enter heaven it must be perfect. Any lack of absolute, total perfection will forever exclude us from the presence of God. Perfect holiness cannot tolerate anything less than perfect holiness. When sin defiled Eden, Eden was forever destroyed. God's law requires a perfect obedience from man and threatens any lack of perfection with death. The law required a perfect sacrifice for atonement. Even God's own dear Son, when he was made to be sin for us, was forsaken by God and slain. God requires perfection. Heaven is a world of perfection. Defilement, abomination, and deceit shall never enter into it. Sin shall never darken the kingdom of light. Sin shall never defile the city Beautiful.

It is only right that all evil be excluded from heaven. It is not at all a matter of bigotry or harshness to declare that heaven shall never be defiled by sin. It is only a matter of righteousness and justice to which every rational man must give assent. Everything in heaven, everyone in heaven, and everyone going to heaven is in full agreement with this decree, 'There shall in no wise enter into it anything that defileth.' We have seen what sin has done to the world of the angels, the physical world, and our fallen race. We would not see heaven ruined by it.

The essence of heaven's bliss is the total absence of sin in that blessed estate.

God's saints in heaven are citizens of a land where there is no sin. We are going to an eternal world, where sin shall never be found. One of heaven's greatest attractions and most cherished glories is total freedom from sin. There we shall enjoy perfect communion with Christ. There we shall have perfect conformity to Christ. There we shall exercise perfect consecration to Christ. Should sin be permitted to enter, all would be ruined! Sin would forever disrupt the peace of heaven, destroy the joy of heaven, and defile the beauty of heaven.

This exclusion of sin from heaven is the exclusion of all who are sinners. 'There shall in no wise enter into it anything that defileth! No person who defiles, no fallen spirit, no sinful man can enter the gates of the New Jerusalem. No tendency to sin, no thought of sin, no will to sin, no desire for sin can go to heaven.

Were it possible for a sinner to go to heaven, he could never enter into the heavenly state. The essence of heaven is a condition, not a place. It is a condition of worship, holiness, and delight in God. If a sinner could get to the place of heaven, he still could not be in the condition of heaven. He would be out of his element. Heaven would be misery for him, if he should enter it in his natural condition of sin, rebellion, and enmity against God.

Our own hearts must give full assent to this exclusion. 'There shall in no wise enter into it anything that defileth.' If I might enter into heaven as I am at this moment with my sinful heart and nature, it would be a horrible crime for me to do so; for my presence there would defile the city of God. A man with a highly contagious deadly disease should never be allowed to mingle with healthy people in society, lest his disease infect everyone. Sanity demands such carriers of death be quarantined.

This exclusion of sin from heaven is the absolute exclusion of all who defile, make abomination, or make a lie. John is telling us that sinners of every kind must be forever excluded from the paradise of God. 'There shall in no wise enter into it anything that defileth.' No evil thoughts, words, or deeds shall enter heaven. Those who enter the city of God must be free from all these things. If we are defiled in any way by sin we cannot enter heaven. No unclean thing shall enter the temple of God (Isaiah 52:1). However, the exclusion goes far beyond moral corruptions. It reaches the spiritual corruptions of Babylonian religion.

'There shall in no wise enter into it anything that worketh abomination.' Abomination in the scriptures usually refers to idolatry, the making of idols, the worship of idols, and the service of idols (1 Kings 11:4-8). The most abominable thing in this world in the sight of God is false religion, idolatry! If your religion is false, if you worship strange gods, you cannot go to heaven. A strange god is a god who wants to save, but lacks the power to do so without the aid and assistance of man. A strange god is a god who sends people he loves to hell. A strange god is a god whose will is frustrated, whose purpose is defeated, whose power is limited. A strange god is a god who sacrifices his own dear Son for many who shall never taste his grace!

'There shall in no wise enter into it anything that maketh a lie.' All false prophets and false teachers, inventors and perpetrators of religious lies shall be damned (1 Timothy 4:1, 2; 2 Thessalonians 2:11, 12). I say this because it simply must be said, every preacher of free-will salvation, every preacher of works religion, every preacher of conditional grace, of whatever sect or denomination is included in this exclusion. Hear this very solemn warning. Realize its meaning and lay it to heart. 'There shall in no wise enter into it anything that defileth, neither whatsoever worketh abomination, or maketh a lie.'

A Reasonable Deduction
In the light of these things, I set before you a plain, obvious, and reasonable deduction. The deduction is just this. None of us can, by any possibility, enter heaven in our present condition. You who are without Christ are without hope (Ephesians 2:11-13). You cannot go to heaven as you are. Should you die without Christ, there would be no hope of you being saved. There is no promise of mercy for you.

Heaven: Who Shall Enter In?

There is no covenant of grace for you. There is no blood atonement for you. There is no pardon for you. There is no hope of life for you. All these things are in Christ, but you are without Christ. And being without Christ, you are without hope.

That which we have seen in the Word of God most certainly slays forever all hope of self-salvation (Jeremiah 13:9). Can a sinful man wash away his own sins? Can a dead man give himself life? Can a guilty man make righteousness for himself? Can a wicked man purge his own heart? If any of us are saved, we must be saved by God and by grace (Ephesians 2:8).

Even those of us who are saved by the grace of God must undergo a great change before we can enter into heaven. Many are of the opinion God's saints in this world get riper and riper for heaven in progressive holiness and sanctification, until at last they are ready for heaven. That simply it is not so. No saved sinner ever imagines he is attaining greater holiness! Long after God had saved him, and after many years of faithful service in the cause of Christ, the Apostle Paul described himself as the very chief of sinners in whom no good thing dwelt (1 Timothy 1:15; Romans 7:18). Our only holiness is Christ, without whom no one shall ever see the Lord (1 Corinthians 1:30; Hebrews 12:14). Before we can enter into heaven we must drop this robe of flesh in death and be transformed into his likeness.

A Blessed Hope
Yet, John gives us, by divine inspiration, a blessed word of hope. We have seen that nothing evil will ever enter heaven, nothing and no one who defiles, works abomination, or makes a lie shall enter heaven. No one has the right to enter by nature. And no one can ever earn the right to enter. Yet there is hope. God has written a book of election, and all whose names are written in that book shall enter in.

No one shall enter into heaven 'but they which are written in the Lamb's book of life.'

We must know one thing: is our name written in that book? If it is, all is well. If it is not, we must be forever damned. Are our names written there? This is certain, if our names are written there, they were written there in eternity, written there because of a covenant, and written there permanently. The Lamb's book of life is the book of God's election. It is the record of redemption by the blood of the Lamb. It is the promise of eternal life, which God, who cannot lie, promised in Christ before the world began.

Let me speak personally. I trust you who read these lines can personally relate to what I am about to say. Yes, my name is written in that blessed book. I know it is because I trust the Lord Jesus Christ, and trusting Christ, I have life. By God's free grace in him, I have all God requires for entrance into heaven (Colossians 1:12; 2:9, 10). He is my worthiness before God. I am complete in him. In Christ, I have atonement for all my sin (Romans 5:10). In Christ, I have perfect righteousness. His righteousness has been imputed to me in justification and imparted to me in sanctification. How can I speak with confident assurance about such great, weighty, eternal matters? I believe God. Faith in Christ is the substance of my hope, the evidence of God's grace in me, and the solitary basis of my assurance before God (Hebrews 11:1; 1 John 5:1-13). Because I trust him, in Christ, I am assured of a glorious change. When death comes, when I am absent from the body I shall be immediately present with the Lord (2 Corinthians 5:1-9). Then, when Christ comes again, I shall be transformed into his image in resurrection glory in the totality of my being (1 Corinthians 15:51-58).

Will you, or will you not, enter into heaven at last? No one will enter into heaven at last who does not enter in by faith in Christ now. He alone can give life to you. Christ alone can pardon our sins. Only

Heaven: Who Shall Enter In?

Christ can make the defiled undefiled, the unrighteous righteous, and sinners saints. May God grant you faith in Christ.

The race of God's anointed priests
Shall never pass away;
Before His glorious face they stand,
And serve Him night and day.
Though reason raves, and unbelief
Flows on, a mighty flood,
They are, and shall be, till the end
The hidden priests of God.

His chosen souls, their earthly dross
Consumed in sacred fire,
To God's own heart their hearts ascend
In flame of deep desire;
The incense of their worship fills
His temple's holiest place;
Their song with wonder fills the heavens,
The glad new song of grace.

Gerhard Tersteegen

Going Home

And the God of peace shall bruise Satan under your feet shortly. The grace of our Lord Jesus Christ be with you. Amen.

Romans 16:20

Chapter 14

Oh, What A Promise!

Thirty-seven years ago, I had a long bout with cancer. The Lord our God graciously and wisely sent the disease. And he graciously and wisely healed me of the disease. I am thankful both for the experience of it and for God's deliverance from it. But there was a time, twenty years ago, right in the middle of a long, long series of cobalt treatments when neither I nor my doctors knew whether I was more likely to live or to die. I was weaker physically, mentally, and emotionally than I ever imagined I could be.

At that critical hour, a friend sent me a card. It had no comments at all. It did not even say, 'Get well' on it. It simply had a Scripture reference written out on it. I would not have known who sent it, had he not put his return address on it. The card was not even signed. However, when I turned to the text written out on the card and read it, being blessed of God to my heart, it did more for me and gave me greater strength and peace than all the letters, cards, and visits I received from my many friends around the world. Their words were sweet, kind, thoughtful, and greatly appreciated; but God's Word was effectual! That word from God is found in Romans 16:20. I pray that God the Holy Spirit will make it effectual to you as you read these lines, 'And the God of peace shall bruise Satan under your feet shortly. The grace of our Lord Jesus Christ be with you. Amen.'

These studies were borne from my personal experience of God's great goodness in Christ and of the blessed power of his Word to comfort, strengthen, and rejoice the hearts of his saints. They are written for the glory of God and the benefit of his people who, as long as they are in this world, are now greatly oppressed by Satan. As I write, I cannot avoid thinking of dear friends, saints of God, enduing great trials of faith. It may be your own heart is presently being tried, overwhelmed with sorrows, trials, or temptations that seem simply too great to endure. If that is the case, take heart. If you are indeed a believer, if you trust the Lord Jesus Christ, this is God's word to you 'And the God of peace shall bruise Satan under your feet shortly. The grace of our Lord Jesus Christ be with you. Amen.'

The Lord God promises all his elect a sure, speedy, and complete triumph over Satan. Let me show you three things clearly set before us by the Holy Spirit in Romans 16:20.

The God Of Peace

First, the Apostle Paul was inspired by the Holy Spirit to give us a suitable title for our God, 'the God of peace'. This title for God is found nowhere except in the writings of the Apostle Paul. But what a suitable title this is for our God, 'the God of peace' (Romans 15:33; Philippians 4:9; 1 Thessalonians 5:23; Hebrews 13:20).

In the immediate context, Paul is contrasting the work of Satan, which was manifest in strife and division, with the work of God, which is peace. The church at Rome had been enduring great turmoil from men who had, by doctrine contrary to the gospel, created strife and division in the church (vv. 17, 18). 'Only by pride cometh contention.' Pride 'stirreth up strife' (Proverbs 13:10; 28:25). And the proud doctrines of Arminian, freewill, works religion, the proud teachings of self-righteousness and legalism are the things 'contrary to the doctrine' of the gospel which cause divisions and offences in the kingdom of God. Therefore, Paul tells us to mark those who teach such doctrines and avoid them. As we do, 'the God of peace will bruise Satan under' our heels, and the church of God will be at peace. That is the contextual interpretation of Paul's words. Still, I cannot avoid asking, 'Why did the Holy Spirit inspire Paul to give this title to our God?'

God is called, 'the God of peace', because he is the Author, Cause, and Giver of all peace; temporal, spiritual, and eternal. God alone can truthfully declare, 'I make peace' (Isaiah 45:7). Civil peace in the nation is God's gift. Domestic peace in the home is God's work. Spiritual peace in the heart can be given by none but God himself. However, this title for our God arises primarily from the fact he is the Source, Cause, and Giver of that 'peace which passeth understanding', both in his saints and in his church.

His thoughts toward us were 'thoughts of peace' from everlasting (Jeremiah 29:11). The covenant of grace, which secured our salvation from eternity, is a 'covenant of peace' made between God the Father, God the Son, and God the Holy Spirit before the world began (Isaiah 54:10; Ezekiel 34:25; 37:26). Because our heavenly Father is 'the God of peace', he appointed his dear Son to be the Peacemaker between men and God. It pleased God to reconcile all things to himself by Christ (Colossians 1:19-22). The Lord God laid upon his Son the chastisement of our peace (Isaiah 53:5).

It is 'the God of peace' who, by his Holy Spirit, speaks peace to our consciences when the blood of Christ is effectually applied to guilty souls (Hebrews 9:14). We find happiness and satisfaction in this world only to the extent 'the peace of God' rules our hearts and minds (Colossians 3:5). The peace of God is peace which he gives in the believer's heart. It is a peace from God that goes out in every direction to God again. It is the peace of reconciliation to God in Christ, the peace of confident faith in the wisdom and goodness of his providence, the peace of brotherly love, and the peace of a blessed hope with regard to eternity.

A Sure Promise

Second, the Spirit of God inspired Paul to proclaim a sure promise for the tried. This is not a promise to everyone who is tried. When men and women live without faith in Christ, while they live as rebels to God, there are no words of comfort to be found for them or promises of goodness and grace given to them. The promises of God are not for unbelievers. If you are yet a rebel to grace and a rebel against God, there is only two promises from God you can claim as your own, 'The soul that sinneth, it shall die', and, 'Believe on the Lord Jesus Christ, and thou shalt be saved'! Yet this is a sure promise to every tried, tempted, troubled believer, 'the God of peace shall bruise Satan under your feet shortly.'

Victory is sure; and it will come speedily! 'The God of peace shall bruise Satan under your feet shortly.' Yet a little while, and he that shall come will come. When Satan seems to have prevailed, and you are ready to give up, he will come! And when God arises to help, 'He shall bruise Satan under your feet' with utmost speed (Genesis 3:15; Psalm 91:13; Mark 16:18). As Christ, the seed of the woman bruised the serpent's head, so, too, we that are Christ's shall tread Satan under our feet. The Apostle does not say we shall bruise Satan under our feet, but God will do it. Yet, neither does Paul say God will

Oh, What A Promise!

bruise Satan under his feet, but rather, 'the God of peace shall bruise Satan under your feet'!

Do you see what Paul is telling us? Whatever it is by which Satan now accuses you, opposes you, and distresses you, soon he who disturbs your peace shall trouble and molest you no more! If Satan was, for a time, permitted to harass our Master, why not us? Yet, as surely as our Saviour triumphed over him, so too must we! Our Lord Jesus bruised the serpent's head for us at Calvary (John 12:31-33). He conquered Satan and spoiled his house when he saved us by his almighty grace (Matthew 12:29; Mark 3:27). In delivering our souls from troubles and temptations, by which Satan accuses us, disturbs our peace, and harasses us with doubts, fears, and confusion, our God bruises him under our heels (Lamentations 3:21-33). Yet, the promise under consideration is a declaration that you and I shall ultimately prevail over our adversary, the devil. Soon we shall be out of range of the serpent's hiss as well as out of his reach. Grace shall win the day. We are, and must forever be, 'more than conquerors' through the Lord Jesus Christ. Hold out a while longer. Persevere stedfast in the faith. Be patient just a little while longer. 'Stand still and see the salvation of the Lord.' Soon, the Red Sea of your woes will open before you. You will pass through the sea as upon dry land. When you have reached the other side, you will see all your enemies dead upon the shore. Then you will laugh and sing triumphantly the song of Moses and of the Lamb. Soon, very soon, our God shall remove us from the sphere in which Satan operates.

'The God of peace shall bruise Satan under your feet shortly.' Study this promise carefully and understand its doctrine. It is God's promise to every tried, troubled, Satan-harassed believer. Satan is under God's control. He is not a rival to God, but a creature of God's making. He is God's devil. He cannot harm you. He is a roaring lion; but he has neither fangs nor claws. Christ pulled them out at Calvary and bound him with the chain of his sovereign omnipotence (John 12:31; Revelation 20:1-3). The only reason God allows him to roar against us is to keep us clinging to Christ. Soon you will laugh at Satan and sing for joy over all your troubles in this world. You will realize that Satan was never allowed to do anything that did not serve the interests of your immortal soul. He was created for that purpose (Hebrews 1:14); and, though he rebels against it with every fibre of his being, he will serve that purpose.

When the Lord God is done with our old adversary, he will cast him into the pit of fire and brimstone and consign him to the place of everlasting torment. Then, not until then, but then, we shall fully understand this promise 'The God of peace shall bruise Satan under your feet shortly.' What will happen in the meantime? How can we go on with the heartaches and troubles that are crushing upon our souls? You may be thinking, 'I need some help now.' You will find our third lesson in the last sentence of Romans 16:20.

A Blessed Benediction

Here, the Apostle Paul was inspired to write out for us a blessed benediction for the chosen people of God. 'The grace of our Lord Jesus Christ be with you. Amen.' The good-will of Christ is toward you. The good work of Christ shall be in you. If the grace of Christ is toward us, who or what can be against us? What is implied in this blessed benediction of grace? Let me show you these five things, and when I am done, tell me if you are not comforted and encouraged!

1. If grace comes from the Lord Jesus Christ, then Jesus Christ is God, because grace is the gift and operation of God alone (Ephesians 2:8).

2. All who are redeemed by the blood of Christ are supplied with grace from Christ.

Oh, What A Promise!

Would he shed his blood for you and then withhold his grace from you? Never! (Ephesians 1:6). Every redeemed sinner has, in Christ, a rightful, legitimate claim upon all the fulness of God's grace. Forgiving grace, justifying grace, regenerating grace, sanctifying grace, and preserving grace, all grace belongs to all for whom Christ died (Ephesians 1:3).

3. The grace of Christ is sufficient for us to meet our every need in this world, even when Satan buffets us (2 Corinthians 12:9).

4. The grace of God in Jesus Christ will bring us to glory at last. Grace is glory begun. Glory is grace complete. Both are the gifts of our Lord Jesus Christ. 'The Lord will give grace and glory' (Psalm 84:11).

5. The grace of God in Christ is sure to his people and just as sure is heavenly glory, too. 'Amen'!

Amen

That word, 'Amen', refers equally to the title ascribed to God, the promise God will 'bruise Satan under your feet shortly', and the blessing of 'grace and glory' from Christ. To all these things the Holy Spirit says 'Amen'! 'So be it'! 'So shall it be'! 'Amen'! Read the promise this way 'The God of peace, Amen! Shall bruise Satan under your feet shortly, Amen! The grace of our Lord Jesus Christ be with you. Amen!

Going Home

Precious in the sight of the LORD is the death of his saints.

Psalm 116:15

Chapter 15

Precious Deaths

Psalm 116 is one of the great Psalms of David. It is a psalm that flowed from a believing heart, from the heart of that man who was a man after God's own heart. David did not take the words of this psalm from books of theology, or from religious tradition, or sentimental stories. These words flowed from a regenerate, believing spirit. These words arose from David's heart and express his thoughts, emotions, and sentiments. Yet they are also words of divine inspiration, written for our learning, admonition, and consolation. As Peter said, this psalm was written by one of those 'holy men of God', who, 'spake as they were moved by God the Holy Ghost' (2 Peter 1:21). We cannot be reminded too frequently of these two facts: first, all Scripture expresses the thoughts, sentiments, emotions, and personal characteristics of the men who wrote it, yet, second, every word of Holy Scripture is God breathed, inspired by God the Holy Spirit, so that the Volume of Holy Scripture is, in its entirety, the very Word of God (2 Timothy 3:16).

Let me show you nine things God says to us in this 116th Psalm by the pen of his servant David. Then I want to answer some more questions about death.

1. David talks about loving the Lord (v. 1). 'We love him because he first loved us' (1 John 4:19). His love for us precedes our love for him. His love for us infinitely supersedes our love for him. His love for us causes our love for him. Still, this is the true confession of every regenerate, believing heart, 'I love the Lord'! 'We love him'! 'I love the Lord because he heard' my cry for mercy, my prayer for forgiveness, and my supplications of repentance!

2. The psalmist talks with confidence of persevering faith (v. 2). He believed, according to the Word of God, that God gave him faith, kept him in faith, and would keep him in faith. David came to God just like we do, the only way any sinner can come to him, by faith in Christ (Hebrews 11:6).

3. He talks about trouble and sorrow causing him to call upon the name of the Lord (vv. 3, 4). Without question, there is much more in the psalm than I will bring out in this brief study. Yet, the sense of the text is obvious. 'The sorrows of death' are the sorrows wrought in the heart by Holy Spirit conviction (John 16:8-11). 'The pains of hell' are the torments of a self-condemned heart (Luke 18:13). 'Trouble and sorrow' are the struggles of a soul seeking peace with God (Psalm 103). The result of real, Holy Spirit conviction, is always faith in Christ. 'Then called I upon the name of the LORD: O LORD, I beseech thee, deliver my soul.'

4. Next, David talks about the character of God (v. 5). The Lord our God is gracious, righteous, and merciful. He is full of mercy!

5. Then the psalmist speaks of God's unfailing faithfulness (vv. 6-8). 'The Lord preserveth the simple.' That is the single-hearted, the sincere, the believing. 'I was brought low, and he helped me.' He who helped David will help us (Hebrews 4:16). The psalmist

essentially says, 'I will trust him to deliver me now, and in the future, who has delivered me in the past' (vv. 7, 8).

6. In verse nine, David speaks with assurance of a blessed hope. All who trust Christ alone as Saviour and Lord, all who look to him alone for righteousness and acceptance with God have reason to live in the assured anticipation of eternity and heavenly glory with Christ (2 Timothy 1:12; Psalm 23:6).

7. In verses 10 and 11, this man after God's own heart talks in one breath about faith, confession, and affliction. These three things always go hand in hand. All who trust Christ confess him as their Lord and confess their faith in him as the only Way, Truth, and Life. And all who confess that the Christ of God, as he is revealed in the Scriptures, is the only Saviour of sinners will suffer for their faith.

8. In the latter part of the psalm, David seems to direct all his thoughts to the worship of the great, gracious God of salvation. He speaks of gratitude (v. 12), commitment to Christ (v. 13), public worship and praise (vv. 14, 17, 18, 19), and the believer's voluntary surrender and consecration (vv. 16-18).

9. Right in the middle of his talk about worship, David talks about precious deaths. 'Precious in the sight of the LORD is the death of his saints' (v. 15). While the Bible speaks of many things as being precious, it only reveals two things that are precious in God's sight. His Son is precious (1 Peter 2:4). His people are precious (Isaiah 43:4). As far as God is concerned, everything about his people is precious; and that fact is precious to me. 'The redemption of their soul is precious' (Psalm 49:8). Their lives are precious (Psalm 72:14). And 'Precious in the sight of the Lord is the death of his saints.'

What is death? You could get many answers to this question. To the family, death means a vacant place, a loved one gone. To the physician, it is a patient lost. To the biographer, it is the last chapter, the book finished. To the newspaper, it is a spot in the obituary, or a brief story, maybe. To the insurance company, it is a payment claimed. To the theologian, death is the separation of the soul from the body. However, when we think about death, either our own death or the death of a friend or loved one who has just passed away, none of those factual answers satisfy us. What is death? Here are four answers to that question. This is one thing we are all going to experience much sooner than we imagine.

Death is the result of sin. 'By one man sin entered into the world, and death by sin' (Romans 5:12). 'The wages of sin is death' (Romans 6:23). There is no greater proof for the biblical doctrine of original sin than the universal fact of death. All die because all are guilty. All die because all are sinners.

Death is an act of God. 'The Lord killeth and the Lord maketh alive.' It does not matter what the secondary cause of a person's death is, the first cause is God (Job 14:1-5).

Death is the decay of the body and return of the soul to God. The body returns to the earth from which it came and the soul to God, who gave it. Whether that soul meets God in judgment or in mercy is not the issue being considered here. The fact is all men die. Soon, you and I must meet God. The prophet of old spoke faithfully 'Prepare to meet thy God'! Meet him we shall, very shortly.

Death is the end of life on earth and the beginning of an eternal existence. Life after death is not a supposition. It is not a superstition. Life after death is a fact, a fact so thoroughly stamped upon the human conscience that it simply cannot be erased (Matthew 25:46; Hebrews 9:27).

This is what death is: the result of sin; an act of God; the decay of the body; and the return of the soul to God with the beginning of an eternal existence. Yet, the Holy Spirit says, 'Precious in the sight of the Lord is the death of his saints.' So I cannot help asking this second question ...

Precious Deaths

What makes the death of a believer precious? All believers are saints, people who have been sanctified. We were chosen to holiness in election (Jude 1), declared holy in redemption and justification (Hebrews 10:10, 14), and actually made holy in regeneration by God the Holy Spirit imparting to us a new nature (2 Peter 1:4; 1 John 3:5-9). This is our threefold sanctification by the grace of God. When a saint dies God looks upon his death as a precious thing. Why?

The death of God's saints is precious in his sight because God does not see things the way we do. 'The Lord seeth not as man seeth.' It is difficult for us to talk about death being precious because everything we see and know is limited by our experience here. God sees things as they really are. He knows that for his saints death is not a loss in any sense at all, but only great gain (Philippians 1:21). Death for us is not a penalty, but a promotion. Death is not the end of life, but the beginning. 'To die is gain', says Paul. To lose a weak, mortal body is to gain an immortal, everlastingly strong body. To leave this world of sin is to enter the heavenly world of perfect righteousness. To drop this house of clay is to enter our house not made with hands in Immanuel's glory land. To leave this temporary state is to enter an eternal state. To leave this world of sorrow is to enter the world of endless, heavenly bliss with Christ. 'To die is gain'!

The death of God's saints is precious to him because the blood that redeemed them is precious to him. We belong to God by the blood atonement of his dear Son. We have been reconciled to God by Christ's precious blood. As our Surety he received his elect from the Father as a trust in the covenant of grace (Ephesians 1:12). As our Redeemer he received his ransomed ones from the law as a purchased possession (Galatians 3:13). As our Saviour the Lord Jesus receives each of his chosen, ransomed ones at the appointed time of love and grace from the Father by the gift of God the Holy Spirit (John 6:37-

40). Christ the King shall receive all his people in resurrection glory by his power. Christ our Priest receives the chosen, one by one, when they are called from earth to heaven in death, as the Father's answer to his intercessory prayer (John 17:24).

'Precious in the sight of the Lord is the death of his saints' because his saints are precious to him! (Jeremiah 31:3; John 13:1; 1 Corinthians 2:9). He has done wonderful things for us in election, redemption, justification, regeneration, and sanctification. He is doing wonderful things for us in preservation and providence. Yet, our God has wonderful things in store for us which no eye has seen, no ear has heard, and no mind has conceived. He has wonderful things yet to show us (1 Corinthians 13:10-13). He has wonderful things yet to give us (John 14:1-3). He has wonderful things yet to do with us (Ephesians 2:7).

This statement applies to all believers. It is an unlimited, unqualified, unconditional statement of truth with regard to all God's saints. 'Precious in the sight of the Lord is the death of his saints.' It matters not who the saint is. We can understand how that the death of a martyr like Stephen would be precious in God's sight. Yet, his death was no more precious than that of the most insignificant saint. All believers have the same attending angels to carry them into paradise, the same Saviour waiting their arrival in heaven, and the same glorious inheritance with Christ (Romans 8:17).

It matters not when the believer dies. We talk of untimely deaths, and accidents, and of lives ending prematurely; but there are no untimely deaths. Every believer's life is a completed, fulfilled plan. God takes his saints when it pleases him, at the time he has appointed. Our Master plucks the grapes of his vineyard when they are ripe and ready to be taken. He never picks green fruit and never leaves his fruit to rot on the vine. With regard to every believer, the hymn writer was correct, when he wrote ...

Precious Deaths

Mortals are immortal here
Until their work is done.

It matters not where the believer dies. It may be in a lonely
hospital room. It may be on a busy highway. It may be upon a terrible
battlefield. It may be in his own bed. That does not matter. 'Precious
in the eyes of the Lord is the death of his saints.' Years ago, an old
preacher in England rose one Sunday morning and announced a
hymn, giving out the first verse like they used to do ...

Father, I long, I long to see
The place of thine abode,
I'd leave these earthly courts and flee
Up to thy throne, O God.

Then he closed his eyes, slipped down behind his pulpit, and died.

Let me go a step further. It does not matter by what means the
believer dies. I have known some to die in very odd circumstances
and by very strange means. I have known many to die suddenly,
without warning. I have seen others die very slow, lingering, painful
deaths. No matter how a believer dies, he dies by God's appointment,
by God's hand, and his death is precious in God's sight.

What about the death of the unbeliever? There is nothing at all
pleasant, comforting, or precious about the death of an unbeliever. I
once knew a young lady whose father died in a state of rebellion and
unbelief. As she stood by his coffin broken-hearted, almost everyone
who came by said to her, 'Well, your daddy is better off now.' After
hearing that statement countless times, the young lady finally said to
one, 'He's in hell now! Do you call that better off?' The unbeliever's
death is a horror, a tragedy, an indescribable woe. God says, 'Blessed

are the dead which die in the Lord'! We cannot write blessed where God has written cursed; and we cannot write cursed where God has written blessed. 'If you die in your sins,' our Saviour said, 'Ye cannot come where I am.' Yet, to every believer, he says, 'Where I am, there you (will) be also.' The hymn writer Isaac Watts wrote,

> When I can read my title clear
> To mansions in the skies;
> I'll bid farewell to every fear
> And wipe my weeping eyes.
>
> Should earth against my soul engage,
> And fiery darts be hurled,
> Then I can smile at Satan's rage,
> And face a frowning world;
>
> Let cares like a wild deluge come
> And storms of sorrow fall,
> May I but safely reach my home,
> My God, my heaven, my all!
>
> There shall I bathe my weary soul
> In seas of heav'nly rest,
> And not a wave of trouble roll
> Across my peaceful breast.

'Precious in the sight of the Lord is the death of his saints.' 'Blessed are the dead which die in the Lord.' That is what God says. The world says, 'Blessed are the rich, the famous, the healthy, and the honoured.' The world takes you into its lavish, luxurious club.

Precious Deaths

There men and women are laughing, singing, and dancing. The room is filled with earthly joy. Nothing is beyond the reach of the rich and the mighty. Autographs are sought from smiling heroes. The best is none too good for those whom the world calls blessed. But all is vanity, a puff of wind, nothing more.

Now, go into a darkened room. There is complete silence. A wife sits by the bed of a dying husband and holds his hand. The children stand around the foot of the bed. Tears run silently down their cheeks. Only the ticking of the clock can be heard. For a brief moment the man opens his eyes widely, a smile crosses his face, and he breathes deeply for the last time. His spirit is gone. Of that man, God says, 'Blessed! Blessed'! You cannot write cursed where God writes blessed; and you cannot write blessed where God writes cursed!

> Someday the silver cord will break,
> And I no more as now shall sing,
> But oh the joy when I awake
> Within the palace of the King.
>
> Someday my earthly house will fall,
> I cannot tell how soon t'will be
> But this I know My all in all
> Has now in heaven a place for me!
>
> Someday, till then, I'll watch and wait,
> My lamp all trimmed and burning bright,
> That when my Saviour opens the gate,
> My soul to him will take its flight.

Frances J. Crosby

Going Home

And they shall see his face; and his name shall be in their foreheads.

Revelation 22:4

Chapter 16

Face To Face With Christ Our Saviour

Heaven is set forth in the Scriptures by many pictures of the bliss awaiting God's elect in eternity. Heaven is a place prepared for us. It is the everlasting kingdom. It is eternal glory. Heaven is our purchased inheritance. It is the city of God and of the Lamb. It is our home. Heaven is our final resting place. These, and many other descriptive phrases, fill our hearts with joy and anticipation. However, surely this is the greatest bliss of the eternal state, the most wondrous consummation of glory, and the very heaven of heaven, 'And they shall see his face'. When the Lord said to Moses, 'Thou canst not see my face and live', he was speaking to a mere mortal upon the earth. Those words have no reference to those who have put on immortality and incorruption. In the coming glory-land every child of God shall see the face of our God and live. Indeed, it is this sight of Christ which shall be the essence and excellence of our life. We shall see him who is the brightness of the Father's glory and the express image of his person face to face! That is the heaven which awaits us!

> Face to face with Christ my Saviour,
> Face to face, what will it be;
> When with rapture I behold him,
> Jesus Christ who died for me?

> Carrie Ellis Breck

The Heavenly Vision

What is this heavenly vision? Some people have very carnal and unscriptural ideas about heaven. Some think of heaven only as a place where they can gratify their carnal desires. They seem to think only of the comforts and pleasures heaven might bring to them in a natural, physical way. To them, the streets of gold, the gates of pearl, and the walls of jasper are enough. I have even heard men talk about heaven as though it were a place that would gratify their religious pride and self-righteousness. Some religious denominations have the vain imagination that their particular brand of religion will give them a place of superiority in glory. In pride and self-righteous bigotry, they suppose all of God's saints will be beneath them and serve them!

Such carnal ideas of heaven must be rejected. However, there are many things in heaven that we shall see and enjoy. We shall see the holy angels who have ministered to us throughout our earthly pilgrimage (Hebrews 1:14). Men and women of flesh and bones will commune with cherubim and seraphim. Gabriel, and all the heavenly hosts, will be known by us. We shall see the patriarchs who served God in those early days of time. We shall even know those men and women who walked with God before the flood like Abel, Enoch, and

Noah. The apostles and prophets will be seen and known by us. Those martyrs, with whose blood the pages of church history are written, will be seen. Those brethren, with whom we have enjoyed sweet fellowship upon the earth, will be seen by us. And those loved ones who fell asleep in Christ Jesus will be seen again. Without question, in our glorified state, earthly ties will no longer divide us; but the saints in glory will know one another, just as Peter, James, and John knew Moses and Elijah when they appeared with them in the mount of transfiguration.

Yet, for all of this, the greatest joy and fulness of heaven will be the fact we shall see Christ himself face to face. What we desire above all else in heaven is the sight of Christ. With the Psalmist we most gladly declare, 'Whom have I in heaven but thee? And there is none upon earth that I desire beside thee' (Psalm 73:25). Christ is all in all to us here, and we long for a heaven in which he shall be all in all to us forever. Here upon the earth, it was a sight of Christ which first turned our sorrow into joy. The daily renewal of communion with Christ lifts us up above the cares of this world. Even here, we say, if we have Christ we have enough. If Christ is all to us now, what will he be in glory? The paradise of God is a heaven of intense, eternal, spiritual fellowship with Christ. Heaven is a place where it is promised, 'They shall see his face.' Moses, we are told, saw his back parts. He saw the train of his majesty; but, there, we shall see his face.

We shall literally see our Saviour's face. Though he is glorified, that very man who died at Calvary is upon the throne of glory. We shall see him, the God-man. What a sight it will be for redeemed sinners. We shall see our well-beloved; his hands, his feet, his side, his head, and his face. We shall literally see him who loved us and gave himself for us.

Even sweeter is the fact we shall enjoy a perfect, spiritual sight of our Redeemer. This text seems to imply a greater ability in the next world by which we shall be able to more fully see Christ. Here, upon the earth, the very best of us are only infants. Now, we know in part. Now, we see through a shaded glass. In heaven, we shall see the Saviour face to face. And we shall know even as we are known. We shall see Christ in such a way as we shall know him. We shall know the height, depth, length, and breadth of the love of Christ that passes knowledge.

We shall see the Saviour always. The saints in heaven shall never cease to see him. We shall never cease to embrace our Saviour! It is not so now. Sometimes we are near the throne, at other times we are afar off. Sometimes we are as bright as the angels, at other times we are as dull as lead. At times we are hot with love, at other times we are cold with indifference. But, the day will soon come, when we shall forever be in the closest possible association with Christ. Then we shall see his face without ceasing. We shall see our Saviour's face as it is now, in the fulness of his glory (John 17:24). John gave us a little glimpse of that in chapter one verses 13-16 of his gospel. Read it again and rejoice in the prospect of this blessed hope.

The word 'see' in this text implies a clear, full, undimmed sight of Christ. We shall see Christ clearly, because everything hindering our sight of him here will be removed. Our sins and our carnal nature will be completely removed. All of those earthly cares that now cloud our vision will be taken out of the way. All our sorrows will be ended (Revelation 21:4). And there, in glory, nothing will stand between us and our Saviour. In heaven there will be no rival in our hearts. We will love Christ supremely.

We shall see Christ personally. Now we see him by faith, but then faith will be turned to sight, and we shall see Christ personally for ourselves. The language of Job is a proper confession of every believer's future prospect. 'For I know that my redeemer liveth, and that he shall stand at the latter day upon the earth: And though after my skin worms destroy this body, yet in my flesh shall I see God: Whom I shall see for myself, and mine eyes shall behold, and not another; though my reins be consumed within me' (Job 19:25-27).

We shall see our Saviour in all the fulness of his person and work. Beholding fully his glorious person, we shall see him who is God over all and blessed forever in the perfection of his glorified manhood. In that day, we shall see Christ in the fulness of his covenant engagements, and in the perfection of all his mediatorial offices as our Surety. We shall see him as our Prophet, Priest, King, Husband, Shepherd, and Substitute. In the world to come, we shall see Christ in the fulness of his saving grace. Then we shall know the meaning of electing love. Then we shall know the price of blood atonement. Then we shall know the power of his priestly intercession. Then we shall know the goodness of his preserving grace.

And when we see his face, our eyes will be full of adoration for him alone. In that world of glory to come there will be no voice heard that speaks of the power of man's free-will, or the goodness of man's works. In that day we shall say, 'Not unto us, not unto us, but unto thy name be honour, and power, and glory, and dominion forever and ever' (Psalm 115:1; Revelation 1:5, 6; 5:9, 10).

Heaven's Joy

Why do we consider this vision of our all-glorious Christ the greatest bliss and joy of heaven? I have said that seeing Christ face to face is the heaven of heaven, the glory of glory. Why do we place such importance upon this one aspect of our eternal inheritance? The answer should be obvious. When we see him our salvation will be complete. Soon the resurrection day will come, and all men will see the great God and Saviour. When the wicked see his face, they will be consumed in his fierce wrath. We shall see him and live. We will be like the burning bush, glowing with the glory of God, but not consumed. We shall stand in the presence of God in perfect salvation. Our souls will be eradicated of every spot of sin. Our bodies will be made immortal, incorruptible, glorious. When we see his face we shall be conscious of his favour and have a perfect and uninterrupted fellowship with him. In glory, we shall walk with God perfectly. When we see his face, and not until we see his face, will we fully know and understand the meaning of being one with him.

When we see him there will be a complete transformation, 'We shall be like him, for we shall see him as he is.' We shall see things as he sees them, think as he thinks, will what he wills, love what he loves, and hate what he hates, perfectly. When we see the face of the Son of God we shall be perfectly satisfied (Psalm 17:15).

The Blessed People

Who are they to whom this promise is given? The apostle tells us those who shall see his face are none, 'but they which are written in the Lamb's book of life' (Revelation 21:27). Every one of those who are the objects of God's eternal grace will see his face. Every soul chosen of God in the council of love will see Christ in the courts of glory (Ephesians 1:4). Every one predestined to be his son will be his son (Romans 8:29) Every soul for whom Jesus died at Calvary will see his face in heaven. They are accepted, pardoned, justified, sanctified, and purchased. And they will see him (Isaiah 53:10-12). Every man, woman, and child who is called by the Spirit of God and regenerated by divine power will see his face (Ephesians 1:13, 14). Everyone that repents of his sin and believes on Christ will see him (John 1:12, 13). Every heart that bows in submission to King Jesus will see the King in his beauty (Luke 14:25-33). Everyone who loves Christ will see Christ (2 Timothy 4:8). They may have been the vilest, most abominable wretches ever to walk upon the earth, but they are washed, they are justified, they are sanctified. And 'they shall see his face'!

They will all with equal clearness see the face of Christ. I read of no secondary joys in heaven. There are no back streets in the New Jerusalem! Whoever invented the doctrine of degrees in heaven knew nothing of free grace! There is as much foundation for such a doctrine in the Scriptures as there is for the doctrine of purgatory, and no more. All the saints of God shall see the Saviour's face. What more can anyone want? The dying thief went with Christ to paradise, and so did Paul. Heaven is altogether the reward of grace, not of debt and heaven will be fully possessed by all the heirs of grace (Romans 8:17). All the saved are loved by God with a perfect love. All were chosen in Christ. We all have the same blessings of grace in the covenant. We are all redeemed by the same blood. We are all accepted in the same righteousness. We are all sons of God upon the same grounds. And we all have the same hope of glory. Heaven was earned and bought for us by the Son of God. It will be given to us in all its fulness. In this world of sorrow, comfort yourself with this hope. 'They' who believe on the Lord Jesus Christ 'shall see his face'.

Going Home

And the ransomed of the LORD shall return, and come to Zion with songs and everlasting joy upon their heads: they shall obtain joy and gladness, and sorrow and sighing shall flee away.

Isaiah 35:10

Chapter 17

Going Home

Recently, I read a sermon by a Scottish preacher named Andrew Gray. He lived from 1633-1656, leaving this world when he was only 23 years old. He was only a very young man when he preached the sermon. The title of his message was 'Returning to Zion'. I cannot tell you when I have read a message that was more delightful, or of a greater blessing to my soul. It was so good that I read it several times. Let me share with you some of the things I gleaned from his message. I hope my gleanings will be a blessing to you, and inspire you to think with joyful anticipation about going home to God our Saviour. I hope these thoughts make you think about heaven and the things awaiting us there. May God the Holy Spirit give us grace to set our hearts upon heaven, where Christ sits on the right hand of God. May our hearts be made to long for those glorious mansions that are yonder provided for us by the Lord Jesus.

A Description

Let me first give you a brief description of heaven according to my own limited understanding of divine revelation. Heaven is a place of rest without rest. This is clear from Hebrews 4:9 and Revelation 4:8.

> 'There remaineth therefore a rest to the people of God.'
> 'And the four beasts had each of them six wings about him; and they were full of eyes within: and they rest not day and night, saying, Holy, holy, holy, Lord God Almighty, which was, and is, and is to come.'

Heaven is a place where the soul is always satisfied yet never satisfied. The psalmist says, and we say with him, 'I shall be satisfied, when I awake with thy likeness'!

There we shall always see God in Christ. Yet, we shall ever want to see more of him. We shall always embrace him, yet want to embrace him more; always feed on him, yet want to feed on him more. In heaven there is both satisfaction and hunger. Heaven is full of mysteries.

Heaven is a place where joy and love eternally flow into our souls, while admiration and praise eternally flow out to our God and Saviour. All the saints' language in heaven is, 'Hallelujah! Praise to the Lamb who sits on the throne.' Oh, what shall it be to be taken within the gates of that blessed city to hear heavenly music? What shall it be to enter into rest, yet never rest from Immanuel's praise? What will it be to be satisfied with great satisfaction yet ever hunger and thirst for Christ without lack of satisfaction?

Heaven's Employment

Second, think for a few minutes about the employment of God's saints in heaven. There are five things to constantly occupy God's saints in heaven; admiration, praise, joy, love, and gazing upon the blessed face of the incarnate God. These activities will occupy God's people as we worship our Saviour, the Lamb who died, the Lion who reigns, the God who is, who was, and who is forever!

There is not a look that is not fixed on our all-glorious Redeemer, the Lord Jesus Christ. Not a movement of the tongue that is not spent in commending Him. Not one step that is not bent on following Christ. Not one stir of the hand that is not occupied in serving Christ. Not one thought that is not filled with Christ. Not one desire that is not full of loving Christ! What makes heaven such a blessed, lovely home? Is it not Christ, who is precious to our hearts? The Lamb is the light of that place (Revelation 21:23). Heaven would be a dark house if Christ were not there. The Lamb of God; crucified, risen, reigning, glorious, he is the light of that house.

Do you see what this means? Heaven is the everlasting world of light, adoration, holiness, perfection and ceaseless worship to which God's saints are rapidly moving. If you only knew the charms of that place it would make you long to join us there in eternity. All the three persons of the Blessed Trinity cry, 'Come up hither'! 'Come up here to us who are here.' All the angels and saints cry, 'Come up here to us who are here.'

Will you be taking up your lodging there? Only if you are made clean every wit; totally righteous, completely holy, and without blame before God by the blood and righteousness of Christ. Only if you are robed in spotless garments of salvation and righteousness by faith in him. Joseph Hart wrote,

> Hail! Thou dear, Thou worthy Lord!
> Holy Lamb! Incarnate Word!
> Hail! Thou suffering Son of God!
> Take the trophies of Thy blood.

What Makes Heaven So Sweet?

And one of the elders answered, saying unto me, What are these which are arrayed in white robes? and whence came they? And I said unto him, Sir, thou knowest. And he said to me, These are they which came out of great tribulation, and have washed their robes, and made them white in the blood of the Lamb. Therefore are they before the throne of God, and serve him day and night in his temple: and he that sitteth on the throne shall dwell among them. They shall hunger no more, neither thirst any more; neither shall the sun light on them, nor any heat. For the Lamb which is in the midst of the throne shall feed them, and shall lead them unto living fountains of waters: and God shall wipe away all tears from their eyes (Revelation 7:13-17).

What Makes Heaven Desirable?

And I looked, and, lo, a Lamb stood on the mount Sion, and with him an hundred forty and four thousand, having his Father's name written in their foreheads. And I heard a voice from heaven, as the voice of many waters, and as the voice of a great thunder: and I heard the voice of harpers harping with their harps: And they sung as it were a new song before the throne, and before the four beasts, and the elders: and no man could learn that song but the hundred and forty and four thousand, which were redeemed from the earth. These are they which were not defiled with women; for they are virgins. These are they which follow the Lamb whithersoever he goeth. These were redeemed from among men, being the firstfruits unto God and to the Lamb. And in their mouth was found no guile: for they are without fault before the throne of God (Revelation 14:1-5).

And I heard a voice from heaven saying unto me, Write, Blessed are the dead which die in the Lord from henceforth: Yea, saith the Spirit, that they may rest from their labours; and their works do follow them (Revelation 14:13).

What Makes Heaven Glorious?

And I saw a new heaven and a new earth: for the first heaven and the first earth were passed away; and there was no more sea. And I John saw the holy city, new Jerusalem, coming down from God out of heaven, prepared as a bride adorned for her husband. And I heard a great voice out of heaven saying, Behold, the tabernacle of God is with men, and he will dwell with them, and they shall be his people, and God himself shall be with them, and be their God. And God shall wipe away all tears from their eyes; and there shall be no more death, neither sorrow, nor crying, neither shall there be any more pain: for the former things are passed away. And he that sat upon the throne said, Behold, I make all things new. And he said unto me, Write: for these words are true and faithful. And he said unto me, It is done. I am Alpha and Omega, the beginning and the end. I will give unto him that is athirst of the fountain of the water of life freely. He that overcometh shall inherit all things; and I will be his God, and he shall be my son. But the fearful, and unbelieving, and the abominable, and murderers, and whoremongers, and sorcerers, and idolaters, and all liars, shall have their part in the lake which burneth with fire and brimstone: which is the second death (Revelation 21:1-8).

What Makes Heaven Exciting?

And I saw no temple therein: for the Lord God Almighty and the Lamb are the temple of it. And the city had no need of the sun, neither of the moon, to shine in it: for the glory of God did lighten it, and the Lamb is the light thereof. And the nations of them which are saved shall walk in the light of it: and the kings of the earth do bring their glory and honour into it. And the gates of it shall not be shut at all by day: for there shall be no night there. And they shall bring the glory and honour of the nations into it. And there shall in no wise enter into it any thing that defileth, neither whatsoever worketh abomination, or maketh a lie: but they which are written in the Lamb's book of life (Revelation 21:22-27).

Heaven's Excellence

Next, let me direct your thoughts, as best I can in this feeble frame, to the excellence of heaven. We know that heaven is a pleasant place. But what makes it pleasant, except that it is a place covered over and filled with the Rose of Sharon and the Lily of the Valley?

What a great sight John had when the angel talked with him and said, 'Come up hither, and I will show you the Bride, the Lamb's wife', and carried him to an exceedingly high mountain, and showed him the holy city, the New Jerusalem (Revelation 21:9, 10).

> And there came unto me one of the seven angels which had the seven vials full of the seven last plagues, and talked with me, saying, Come hither, I will show thee the bride, the Lamb's wife. And he carried me away in the spirit to a great and high mountain, and showed me that great city, the holy Jerusalem, descending out of heaven from God. (Revelation 21:9, 10)

What is it that makes heaven such an excellent place? It is the soul-satisfying vision of God we have there in the person of his dear Son, our Mediator, in all his glory! There we shall see God face to face! It is written, 'They shall see his face'! What could be more excellent and glorious? What could be more rewarding and honouring? What could be more joyous and satisfying?

Here we see Christ dimly, as 'through a glass darkly'. There we shall see him face to face. What will be the Bride's thoughts when Christ first takes her in his arms? Who can imagine such things? 'This is my Beloved! He has brought me now into his banqueting house! His banner over me is love'! Oh, what shall our thoughts be when Christ takes us into his arms? I think we shall fall apart! Oh, what shall it be to be with Christ in heaven?

Six Questions
Here are six questions I must have answered. As I meditate upon the excellence and glory of heaven, I cannot help asking these six questions of my Saviour. I hope you will be asking them as well, as I relate them to you.

Going Home

The first is this: shall this tongue, that has so often taken my Saviour's name in vain and so often polluted the holiness of God, ever be made like the tongues of angels, to express the greatness and glory of Christ?

The second question is this: shall these eyes, that have been the windows through which so many sins have come into my soul, ever see the Spotless One who sits on the throne of glory?

When I see Christ I would blush to look him in the face, were it not for the fact that he has declared 'sorrow and sighing shall flee away'! When we see his face, his transforming face, where shall we turn our eyes? A sight of Christ will make us eternally wonder. Do you not groan, my brother, my sister, for the sight of Christ? Soon, we shall see him as he is!

The third question is this: shall these ears, that have listened to so much foulness and enjoyed so much vanity, ever hear those songs above?

We must hear either the eternal shrieks of the damned in hell or the songs of the choirs of heaven. Oh, how sweetly they sing! For now comfort yourselves with this, the day is coming when you shall no more hang your harps on the willows because you are in a strange land, but you shall eternally cry out, 'Worthy is the Lamb! All praise to him who sits on the throne'!

The fourth question is this: shall these feet of mine, that have pursued endless futility and folly, ever follow the Lamb whithersoever he goeth?

The fifth question I ask is this: shall this heart of mine, which has been a house of many idols, ever be made the unrivalled dwelling-place of my Saviour?

The last question I ask is this: shall these hands, that have been the instruments of so much evil and iniquity, ever embrace and hold that matchless Holy One who sits yonder on the throne?

Going Home

What will we do when we first get Christ in our arms? We might well imagine our first day in heaven will be the most glorious. But that will not be the case. Though we have never seen our Husband before, the longer we are with him in heaven's glory the more we shall love him and the more we shall know his love for us!

What will we discover in glory? There is no outcast there, no desertion, no unbelief, no misunderstanding of Christ, no questioning his wisdom, no doubts about his ways, no misinterpreting of his will, and no displeasure with his purpose. When we go through the gates of the New Jerusalem we shall pass over the graves of desertion, and jealousy, and unbelief, and all our idols, and we shall never return to them!

What a pleasant day it will be when faith and hope shall yield themselves to love and sight. Faith and hope are our attendants here, but love and sight will be our eternal attendants above. Faith and hope fight the battle here, but love and sight will sit at home and divide the spoil in heaven. Faith and hope embrace Christ through the veil, but love and sight embrace him face to face. Soon, we shall leave both faith and hope, but we shall never weep for leaving these dear, blessed companions.

One more thing we will forever leave behind when we leave this world is repentance. In heaven we shall have nothing to repent of!

Six Struggles
Here are six great struggles I have with regard to heaven and going home to my God and Saviour.

I have a constant struggle here with sin, unbelief, hardness of heart, indifference, and spiritual ignorance. I confess, with Agur, 'Surely, I am more brutish than any man, and have not the understanding of a man. I neither learned wisdom, nor have the knowledge of the holy' (Proverbs 30:2, 3).

Still, I am comforted with this: as soon as I enter the gates of that blessed city all my clouds will dissipate immediately. I will never again have a wrong thought of God throughout all eternity. Then, I shall begin to say to myself, 'Is this me, the ignorant and brutish man?'

I am often under much desertion. I never try go to my God in prayer but that I find an absent God, a hidden Christ, and a quenched Spirit. Often, more often than not, I cannot even speak to him in prayer, but only groan before him.

Still I find comfort in this: there is no desertion in heaven. There are none in glory-land who cry, 'How long, Lord, wilt thou hide thy face from me?' (Psalm 13:1). This is almost too much for this sinful soul to grasp, but it is a blessed fact. I cannot tell you how I rejoice in it! In heaven, I shall never again find it hard to speak to my God. I shall never again grow weary of serving him. I shall never again find it difficult to worship and praise and commune with my Beloved!

I must also acknowledge this fact for I do not want to pretend things are different with me than they really are! I want to be honest. I do not want to be a hypocrite! I sometimes struggle hard with assurance. I sometimes question whether I will go home to heaven with Christ when I leave this world, or perish in hell.

How I wish it were not so, but I am often like John Newton when he wrote,

> 'Tis a point I long to know,
> Oft it causes anxious thought,
> Do I love the Lord or no,
> Am I His, or am I not?

Perhaps the struggle itself is horribly evil. Perhaps I should never have the struggle. But I do, and it is real. I often have terribly painful questions concerning the reality of my faith. Oh, how I long to trust Christ perfectly! Completely! Without doubt! Without unbelief! But, even with regard to these things, my God gives me great consolation and hope. It is not the measure of my faith, or the quality of my faith, or the evidences of my faith that gives me hope, but Christ, the solitary Object of my faith! Oh, what comfort there is for my soul in this! There will be no more doubting and unbelief in heaven. When I cross over the threshold of Heaven's Gate, I will bid everlasting, 'Farewell' to all unbelief, doubts and questions!

I have another, painful complaint, a bitterness in my soul that is well nigh unbearable. My love for Christ is so horribly little that I often fear I have no love for him at all.

Yet, bless God, honesty will not allow me to say, horrible thought, I do not love him. Oh, no! When I hear my Saviour say, 'Lovest thou me?' I hang my head with shame, but confess, 'Lord, thou knowest all things; thou knowest that I love thee.' 'We love him, because he first loved us.'

I take great comfort and delight in this: soon, I will love my Saviour perfectly! As soon as these eyes are closed in death, as soon as I have gasped my last breath in this weak, mortal, sinful frame, I will love him who is altogether lovely as he ought to be loved!

Here is another terrible, heavy burden in my soul, a burden from which I find no relief in this world, a burden that makes me a little anxious to go home: so long as I am in this world, I know that I shall never prevail over my many idols, and get them forced out of my heart. I flee idolatry constantly, but can never leave it altogether behind. I struggle to keep myself from idols; but find the struggle a constant, uphill battle.

Still, when I think of going home, when I think of heaven, I find comfort, even in the face of this. All my idols will be slain before I get home. In one day, at once, all shall be slain as I behold the Lord

Jesus standing at the right hand of God to receive me. My Saviour demands all my heart, and deserves it. Blessed be his name, soon he shall have it! In heaven's glory there will be no rival in my heart's affections to him!

And I have another great struggle in my soul: I fear I know very little, if anything, of true prayer. Prayer is often found on my lips; but I often question whether prayer is ever found in my heart! John Burton wrote,

> I often say my prayers
> But do I ever pray?
> And do the wishes of my heart
> Go with the words I say?
>
> I may as well kneel down
> And worship gods of stone,
> As offer to the living God
> A prayer of words alone.
>
> For words without the heart
> The Lord will never hear,
> Nor will He to those lips attend
> Whose prayers are not sincere.
>
> Lord teach me what I need,
> And teach me how to pray;
> Nor let me ask Thy grace,
> Not feeling what I say.

Going Home

In heaven, when I get home, I shall never again have this struggle. Then, I will never again have need of prayer. All my soul's desires will be fully satisfied at once. Then, I shall see my God and Father glorified, my Father's will fully performed, his kingdom come, and my Saviour satisfied. I will forgive even as I am forgiven. I will love even as I am loved. And I shall be like him, when I see him as he is (1 John 3:2).

> As for me, I will behold thy face in righteousness: I shall be satisfied, when I awake, with thy likeness (Psalm 17:15).

> Behold, what manner of love the Father hath bestowed upon us, that we should be called the sons of God: therefore the world knoweth us not, because it knew him not. Beloved, now are we the sons of God, and it doth not yet appear what we shall be: but we know that, when he shall appear, we shall be like him; for we shall see him as he is. And every man that hath this hope in him purifieth himself, even as he is pure (1 John 3:1-3).

The Father, the Son and the Holy Spirit, the three persons of the Blessed Trinity, are each crying out, 'Come up here to us who are here'! And the joys of heaven, if they had a tongue, would cry out, 'Oh, come up here'! And that sweet and blessed transcendence in the face of Christ cries out, 'Come up here'! Does not your soul's need cry out, 'Go up there'!?

Some of us may be in eternity before long; and that is just fine, for eternity is sweet if we go to heaven. I remember a word in Job (Job 9:25) 'My days are swifter than a post; they flee away as the ships.' For the believer death cuts all the cords that tie us to this world, but it makes the everlasting knot that binds us to Christ. Death is our friend. Our death day will be our coronation day.

Someone once said, 'Death is Christ's messenger to bring you home, sent to you either with a letter of commendation to speed you on or with a love letter in his hand to make you shout for joy. Oh, therefore, let us love him and long to be with him.'

> And the ransomed of the LORD shall return, and come to Zion with songs and everlasting joy upon their heads: they shall obtain joy and gladness, and sorrow and sighing shall flee away (Isaiah 35:10).

All the ransomed of the Lord will return and come to Zion. All will return with songs and everlasting joy upon their heads. All will, upon their return, find joy and gladness. 'And sorrow and sighing shall flee away'! Oh, happy, happy, blessed day! Soon, 'sorrow and sighing shall flee away'!

> And I saw a new heaven and a new earth: for the first heaven and the first earth were passed away; and there was no more sea. And I John saw the holy city, new Jerusalem, coming down from God out of heaven, prepared as a bride adorned for her husband. And I heard a great voice out of heaven saying, Behold, the tabernacle of God is with men, and he will dwell with them, and they shall be his people, and God himself shall be with them, and be their God. And God shall wipe away all tears from their eyes; and there shall be no more death, neither sorrow, nor crying, neither shall there be any more pain: for the former things are passed away. And he that sat upon the throne said, Behold,

I make all things new. And he said unto me, Write: for these words are true and faithful' (Revelation 21:1-5).

Amen.

Going Home

Going Home

Jesus our triumphant Head,
Risen victorious from the dead;
To the realms of glory's gone
To ascend His rightful throne.

Cherubs on the Conqueror gaze:
Seraphs glow with brighter blaze;
Each bright order of the sky,
Hail Him as He passes by!

Saints the glorious triumph meet;
See their garments at His feet!
By His fears His toils, are viewed,
And His garments rolled in blood!

Heaven its King congratulates;
Opens wide her golden gates;
Angels, songs of victory sing,
All the blissful regions ring!

Sinners join the heavenly powers,
For redemption all is ours;
None but burdened sinners prove,
Blood-bought pardon, dying love.

Hail! Thou dear, Thou worthy Lord!
Holy Lamb! incarnate Word!
Hail! Thou suffering Son of God!
Take the trophies of Thy blood.

                              Joseph Hart

Going Home

Index Of Bible Verses

Ephesians
1:3	36, 92, 101, 157
1:3, 4	99
1:3-6	118, 119
1:3-9	40
1:4	174
1:6	92, 118, 126, 157
1:7	16, 36
1:9, 10	117
1:10	59
1:10-14	40
1:11	55, 84, 93
1:12	118, 163
1:13	91
1:13, 14	174
1:14	43, 70, 84, 118
1:23	124
2:1-5	17
2:1-9	79
2:6	42
2:7	59, 118, 142, 164
2:8	147, 156
2:8, 9	98
2:11-13	146
3:18, 19	124
3:19	103
4:30	70, 91
5:25-27	16, 21, 101, 142

Philippians
1:6	17
1:21	163
1:21-23	28, 29
1:23	44, 65, 134
3:10	91
4:9	152
4:13	18

Colossians
1:12	55, 94, 148
1:14	16
1:19-22	16, 153
1:21-23	81
1:27	34, 36
2:9	72, 126
2:9, 10	36, 148
2:12	132
3:1-3	103, 120
3:1-4	51, 74
3:5	154

1 Thessalonians
2:12	43, 58
4:13-18	27
4:16	136
5:23	152

2 Thessalonians
2:11, 12	146
2:13, 14	39
2:16	91

1 Timothy
1:15	147
4:1, 2	146
4:8	37
6:12	43

2 Timothy
1:9	98, 99
1:12	83, 137, 161
3:16	159
4:6-8	18, 83, 137
4:7, 8	98
4:8	59, 174

Going Home

Going Home